Learni

Sport in our Society

Series Editor: Cara Acred

Volume 270

Independence Educational Publishers

First published by Independence Educational Publishers

The Studio, High Green

Great Shelford

Cambridge CB22 5EG

England

© Independence 2014

British Library Cataloguing in Publication Data

Sport in our society. -- (Issues ; 270)
1. Sports--Social aspects--Great Britain. 2. Doping in
sports.
I. Series II. Acred, Cara editor.
306.4'83'0941-dc23

ISBN-13: 9781861686893

Printed in Great Britain
MWL Print Group Ltd

Contents

Introduction

Sport in our Society is Volume 270 in the **ISSUES** series. The aim of the series is to offer current, diverse information about important issues in our world, from a UK perspective.

ABOUT SPORT IN OUR SOCIETY

The role of sport in our society is constantly evolving. This book considers sport's interaction with different demographics, its function within society and the controversies surrounding the topic. It also explores the concept of inclusion within sport, looking at issues of gender, disability and religion.

OUR SOURCES

Titles in the **ISSUES** series are designed to function as educational resource books, providing a balanced overview of a specific subject.

The information in our books is comprised of facts, articles and opinions from many different sources, including:

⇨ Newspaper reports and opinion pieces

⇨ Website factsheets

⇨ Magazine and journal articles

⇨ Statistics and surveys

⇨ Government reports

⇨ Literature from special interest groups.

A NOTE ON CRITICAL EVALUATION

Because the information reprinted here is from a number of different sources, readers should bear in mind the origin of the text and whether the source is likely to have a particular bias when presenting information (or when conducting their research). It is hoped that, as you read about the many aspects of the issues explored in this book, you will critically evaluate the information presented.

It is important that you decide whether you are being presented with facts or opinions. Does the writer give a biased or unbiased report? If an opinion is being expressed, do you agree with the writer? Is there potential bias to the 'facts' or statistics behind an article?

ASSIGNMENTS

In the back of this book, you will find a selection of assignments designed to help you engage with the articles you have been reading and to explore your own opinions. Some tasks will take longer than others and there is a mixture of design, writing and research-based activities that you can complete alone or in a group.

FURTHER RESEARCH

At the end of each article we have listed its source and a website that you can visit if you would like to conduct your own research. Please remember to critically evaluate any sources that you consult and consider whether the information you are viewing is accurate and unbiased.

Useful weblinks

www.bps.org.uk

www.chancetoshine.org

www.children1st.org.uk

www.theconversation.com

www.empower2perform.com

www.epigram.org.uk

www.euathletes.org

www.gov.uk

www.nhs.uk

www.nus.org.uk

www.offsiderulepodcast.com

www.onislam.net

www.sportengland.org

www.sportingequals.org.uk

www.thesportinmind.com

www.sportni.net

www.tes.co.uk

www.wada-ama.org

www.yougov.co.uk

www.youngfoundation.org

Sport and society

Sport and young people

Research and project evaluation provides useful evidence on what motivates and deters young people's sporting participation.

Sport has to compete with the many leisure and lifestyle choices available to young people.

A 2012 Sport England review of research in this field found sport needs to adapt to key factors affecting young people's take-up:

⇨ a move towards 'lifestyle' related sports which lack the regulation of traditional sport

⇨ the way social media is breaking down the boundaries between passive interest, doing, playing and watching sport

⇨ psychological factors such as self-confidence, body image and young people's perceptions about their own sport competence

⇨ access to facilities and cost – these play a part, but are secondary to the other factors above.

Life transitions – such as moving from primary to secondary school, and from school to higher education or work – often lead to young people dropping out of sport.

Young women are less likely than young men to enjoy competitive sport. Many young women will respond positively to approaches that favour improvement rather than winning, and to initiatives such as single gender sessions.

Sportivate

Sportivate is a £32 million Lottery programme that gives 14- to 25-year-olds access to six-week courses in a range of sports. Three months after the end of their project, 88.9% were still taking part in sport. The evaluations list critical factors in reaching this group.

Sport and older people

The sporting habit declines with age, but people are often keen to go on exercising with the right support.

Research among recently retired people suggests that the social component, fun and enjoyment of exercise are important motivators.

Its recommendations include:

⇨ positive messages, including reassurances about safety

⇨ taster sessions

⇨ avoid the word 'sport'

⇨ make opportunities as local as possible

⇨ promote the opportunities available to this age group.

Sport and sexual orientation

Sport take-up is high among gay men and lesbian women, according to the latest *Active People Survey*.

Lesbian and bisexual women are more likely to take part in sport than all women – 44% play sport at least once a week, compared to just over 30% of all women according to analysis of *Active People Survey* data in 2012 (APS 6 Q2 results).

Gay men are also more likely than the overall male population to take part in sport, though participation is not as high for bisexual men.

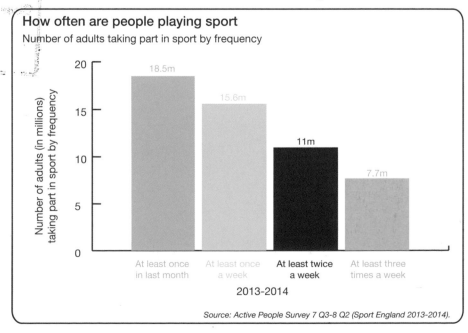

How often are people playing sport

Number of adults taking part in sport by frequency

Number of adults (in millions) taking part in sport by frequency

- 18.5m — At least once in last month
- 15.6m — At least once a week
- 11m — At least twice a week
- 7.7m — At least three times a week

2013-2014

Source: Active People Survey 7 Q3-8 Q2 (Sport England 2013-2014).

The data also reveals that sexual orientation influences the type of sport people take up. Gay and bisexual males are less likely to take part in team sports, while lesbian and bisexual females are more likely to do so.

Research review

Social attitudes and lack of information have hampered policies to ensure an inclusive approach to LGBT (lesbian, gay, bisexual and transgender) people in sport, according to a 2008 literature review commissioned by Sport England and the other UK sports councils.

As a result, some LGBT people have given up sport, or hidden their sexuality.

The report recommended:

⇨ practical guidance for clubs and other bodies on inclusive support for LGBT people

⇨ prepare advice sheets on how to provide for transsexuals and transgendered people in different sports

⇨ leadership training about sexual orientation equality for all key public officials working in sport.

Sport and ethnicity

The number of people playing sport varies widely by ethnic group.

Analysis carried out in 2012 on *Active People Survey* data (APS 6 Q2 results) showed take-up is higher among people from mixed background, with 44% playing sport at least once a week.

Among other ethnic groups, participation varies very little for men. Among women, however, females from white backgrounds are also more likely to take part in sport compared to people from Chinese, other and black backgrounds, with a low of 21% for females from Asian backgrounds.

Across sport as a whole, 89% of those who take part are from white, and 11% from non-white backgrounds (88% of the English population are from white backgrounds). But this varies in specific sports.

In basketball and cricket, for instance, over a third are from non-white backgrounds; badminton and football also have a higher than average proportion of players from these groups. On the other hand, non-white players make up a small share of cyclists and golfers.

Research review

A Sport England review of research in the field found relatively low numbers of people from ethnic minorities in sport. This was true of spectators, volunteers and administrators as well as players.

The paper recommends good practice for sports providers, including:

⇨ training for those working in sport on the needs of other ethnic communities and on challenging exclusion

⇨ ensuring that racial equality objectives in policies are converted into practice

⇨ training sports facilitators from Black and Minority Ethnic (BME) communities.

Sport and faith groups

Faith has an influence on sports take-up, especially among some groups of women.

People who state they have no religion are more likely to take part in sport.

Analysis carried out in 2012 on *Active People Survey* data (APS 6 Q2 results) showed participation is also high among Sikh, Muslim and Buddhist men. But it is much lower for women of the same faiths, compared with the overall female population.

There are also notable differences among different sports. For instance, badminton, basketball and cricket all have higher take-up rates for Buddhist, Hindu, Jewish, Sikh and Muslim faiths as compared with those stating a Christian faith or no religion. In football, however, this rate is the same as for people stating no religion.

Economic conditions

Hard economic times have had a significant impact on the take-up of sport.

A study commissioned by Sport England found that one of the side-effects of recession has been a reduction in the number of people taking part in sport.

Past evidence from the 1980s and 1990s suggests that economic recessions did not have a major effect on sports participation. However, the latest paper found clear evidence that the recession which began in 2008 has had a 'significant negative effect'.

The effect was more pronounced in expensive sports such as sailing, skiing and golf. Sports such as running continued to grow.

⇨ The above information is reprinted with kind permission from Sport England. Please visit www.sportengland.org for further information.

© *Sport England 2014*

Who plays sport?

The national picture

Sport England's data gives an insight into who plays sport and how they play it.

Sport England's data for 2013/14 shows that:

⇨ 15.6 million adults now play sport at least once a week. That's 1.7 million more than in 2005/6

⇨ In addition, over 900,000 14–15-year-olds play sport at least once a week

⇨ Most adults – 52% – still do not play sport

⇨ 17.4% of adults now take part in at least three sport sessions a week – up from 15.5% in 2005/6

⇨ There has been a statistically significant increase in six out of the nine English regions from 2005/6 to 2013/14.

Who plays sport?

The number of adults who play sport at least once a week is on the rise – but just over half of all adults play no sport.

There are a number of key factors in sports participation:

Gender

Gender has a big influence on sports take-up. More men play sport than women. Currently 40.9% of men play sport at least once a week, compared to 30.3% of women. At a younger age, men are much more likely than women to play sport. But this difference declines sharply with age.

Age and socio-economic groups

Age is a factor in participation: 54.5% of 16- to 25-year-olds (58.0% of 14–25-year-olds) take part in at least one sport session a week, compared to 32.0% of older adults (age 26-plus).

Take-up is highest among managerial/professional workers and intermediate social groups. It is lowest among manual workers and unemployed people.

Ethnicity and disability

The number of both black and minority ethnic and white British adults playing sport is increasing. More disabled people are taking part in sport – latest results show 17.8% are playing sport regularly, up from 15.1% in 2005/6.

How do people take part?

As well as playing sport, the *Active People Survey* data shows how people are involved in sport – for instance, through club membership, tuition or coaching, through competitive sport or as volunteers.

⇨ Over 9.2 million people (16-plus) are members of a sports club – 21% of the English population.

⇨ Around 7.3 million people (16-plus) received sports coaching in 2013/14, while 5.7 million took part in competitive sport. Both activities have declined since 2005/6.

⇨ There are also over 2.9 million people (16-plus) who volunteer regularly in sport, according to the latest figures.

By sport

Examine the popularity of different sports and how people engage with them – whether through organised competitions, club membership, or tuition.

Who plays sport?

Swimming, athletics, cycling, and football are amongst the most popular sports in 2013/14:

⇨ Over 2.9 million people were swimming once a week in 2013/14, making it the top sport by a significant margin.

⇨ The number of people taking part in athletics weekly has risen from 1.4 million in 2005/6 to over 2.1 million today.

⇨ The number of weekly cyclists is also over 2.1 million, while football is part of the weekly routine for over 1.9 million people.

Other sports becoming more popular – though from a lower base – include boxing and table tennis.

How do people take part?

Sports clubs

Club membership is most common in rugby union and hockey. Over half of those who take part in these sports belong to clubs.

Relatively few people are club members in sports such as athletics (4.7%), swimming (3.1%) and cycling (2.1%).

Club membership has remained fairly static in most sports since 2007/8.

Tuition

More than half of all those taking part in rugby union and hockey have had tuition in their sport.

Since 2007/8, tuition rates have fallen in basketball, canoeing and kayaking, cricket and snowsports. Tuition in swimming has increased.

Competition

More than half of those who take part in hockey and rugby union are involved in competition, as are just under half who play netball. Swimmers and cyclists are least likely to compete, but the number of competitive cyclists is growing.

A number of sports have seen changes in competition rates since 2007/8. There have been declines in sports, including football.

⇨ The above information is reprinted with kind permission from Sport England. Please visit www.sportengland.org for further information.

Move it: increasing young people's participation in sport

London 2012 presented an opportunity to showcase British sport. Billions of pounds were invested in developing the state-of-the-art facilities in which the world's greatest athletes competed for Olympic glory. Millions of people cheered them on; billions tuned in to watch. However, while the numbers of people watching sport seems to know no bounds, fewer and fewer people are engaging in physical activity themselves. Sedentary behaviour is becoming the new norm.

This epidemic of physical inactivity represents a serious problem to society. Poor health outcomes cost the NHS and the broader economy. Inactivity is estimated to cost the whole economy over £8 billion a year. There is an urgent need to reverse the current trends and start increasing levels of sports and physical activity. All the evidence suggests that raising levels of activity and participation in sports not only improves health outcomes, but has other positive social effects including reducing crime, improving mental health and well-being, increasing educational attainment, and can result in more cohesive communities.

Significant changes are required to Britain's sporting infrastructure to increase the numbers of people,

and particularly young people, participating in sporting activity, rather than simply watching it. We welcome Sport England's 2012–17 strategy, but believe far more radical change needs to happen to change policy, funding and the organisation of sport in order to reverse the growing levels of inactivity among young people. We have proposed a four-point plan:

1. Youth-centred sports policy

⇨ Place young people at the centre of policy making

⇨ Re-direct funding away from elite and competitive sports

⇨ Leverage digital platforms to help drive behavioural change

2. Co-ordinated delivery of sport

⇨ Cross-departmental physical activity strategy

⇨ Re-prioritise physical activity in schools

⇨ Co-ordinate and open up delivery and provision at the local level

3. Leverage current funding streams and align new ones

⇨ Align current investments

⇨ Maximise corporate investment

⇨ Unlock informal resources

⇨ Build a better business case for investment in physical activity

4. Data tracking and accountability to make sport count

⇨ Consolidate existing measurement systems

⇨ Recognise physical activity as an outcome

⇨ Install mechanisms for monitoring and accountability

This plan would begin to change behaviour in England. But we are not the only country that would benefit from a new approach. Nearly all developed countries, and many developing ones, are facing the same issues. There are no universal answers. Solutions have to respond to the social, economic, political and cultural context in each country. However, in order to achieve success we need to share and learn from each other's experiences. Physical inactivity is a global challenge and can only be fully addressed if countries act locally, but also co-ordinate efforts, work together and learn from each other.

⇨ The above information is reprinted with kind permission from The Young Foundation. Please visit www.youngfoundation.org for further information.

Developing good moral character and self-esteem in youth sport

The influence of youth sport development programmes and coaches in the development of good moral character and self-esteem.

By Shameema Yousuf

Whilst the UK tends to follow a model of sports specialisation and performance-focused athlete environments (Johnston, Harwood & Minniti, 2013), youth development sports programmes can lead to positive development of young people and promote healthy, satisfying and productive lifestyles (Hamilton, Hamilton & Pittman, 2004). They have been found to improve youth quality of life and simultaneously enhance development of personal and social skills that prepare youth for adulthood (Fraser-Thomas, Cote & Deakin, 2005).

Self-esteem is linked closely to an adolescent's perception of competence. They gain this through comparison against their peers and by being evaluated by their peers (Horn & Weiss, 1991). In the sports context, youth athletes determine their ability against peers on their own team, as well as against the opposing team (Ewing, Gano-Overway, Branta & Seefeldt, 2002).

During the ages of ten to 24, adolescents are developing cognitive, social and emotional skills equipping them with essential skills to navigate adulthood (University of Minnesota extension, 2012). During these ages, young people also go through maturation changes which result in issues with personal identity, moral self and emotional independence. Sport has the potential to contribute to self-esteem and moral development. Self-esteem is linked closely to an adolescent's perception of competence. They gain this through comparison against their peers and by being evaluated by their peers (Horn & Weiss, 1991). In the sports context, youth athletes determine their ability against peers

on their own team, as well as against the opposing team (Ewing, Gano-Overway, Branta & Seefeldt, 2002).

In developing self-esteem, coaches who engage positive reinforcement, frequent encouragement and corrective feedback can improve on a youth's self-esteem (Smith, Smoll & Curtiss, 1979). The coaches' involvement is critical to the development of self-esteem as their level of competence can be assessed more accurately. The appropriateness of coaches' feedback is also critical in that it may not be appropriate to reward a child whose effort was lacking by giving positive feedback. Instead, by giving constructive criticism with positive reinforcement in response to performance errors, a player's perception of competence can be built.

Sports also provide an opportunity to develop moral values and positive behaviour. Sport activities allow participants to demonstrate values such as working hard, playing fair, playing by the rules of the game, and appropriate behaviour towards others such as good sportsmanship (Shields & Bredemeier, 1995). However, whilst the opportunity to develop moral values does exist through sport participation, it should be noted that participation in sport can also undermine the moral development of youth if it solely focuses on physical activity. That is, moral behaviour can be learnt from engaging with others or by one being taught ethical behaviour. Tae Kwon Do is a sport that emphasises physical skills alongside the philosophy of the

sport which includes reflection and meditation. In one particular study youths involved in the sport experienced lower levels of anxiety and aggression, increased self-esteem and improved social skills in comparison to those students who were trained only in self-defence physical skills (Trulson, 1986).

When it comes to morality, developing programmes which are led by coaches and parents that promote fair play, focus on personal improvement such as working hard, co-operating with others and becoming good citizens (Duda, 1989) will develop athletes who display good sportsmanship in contrast to those more concerned with beating others at all costs. Coaches can teach their youth appropriate behaviours when certain situations arise in games and practice, and by displaying moral behaviours as instructors.

How to avoid negative sports environments

Sports environments can also very quickly lead to young adolescents making incorrect assessments of their abilities by observing peers and making social comparisons. This results in their self-esteem being threatened (Festinger, 1954). With those who have their self-esteem at stake, downward social comparisons to protect against negative self-evaluation can result in lost interest in the sport. The early involvement of coaches and parents is therefore imperative for the development of accurate assessments of abilities and competence.

Although there is an argument for moral development through sports, there has also been evidence to suggest that sports can increase the risk of opportunities for unstructured social activities, substance abuse and non-violent aggressive behaviour (Gardner, Roth & Brooks-Gunn, 2011).

Therefore, it is essential that coaches and administrators consider the following factors that foster moral values, build self-esteem, develop social connectedness, as well as develop emotional, intellectual and physical growth (Morris, Sallybanks, Willis & Makkai, 2003):

⇨ Scaffolding through coach and peer relationships to allow for skill building

⇨ Positive reinforcement and appropriate constructive learning

⇨ Empowering adolescents to be a part of the decision-making process

⇨ Fostering inclusion rather than an exclusive dynamic

⇨ Fostering self-improvement rather than self-comparison

⇨ Provide community-serving opportunities

⇨ Allowing each youth to have an important role and voice

⇨ Encourage social development alongside physical development

⇨ Relating to the youth how the skills and efforts acquired in such environments are transferred to other domains.

References

Duda, J.L. (1989). The relationship between task and ego orientations and the perceived purpose of sport among male and female high school athletes. *Journal of sport and exercise psychology*, 4, 24-31.

Ewing, M.E., Gano-Overway, L.A., Branta, C.F. & Seefelt, V.D. (2002). The role of sports in youth development. In Parodoxes of youth and sport edited by Gatz, M., Messner, M.A. and Ball-Rokeach, S.J. (2002).

Festinger, L. (1954). A theory of social comparison, *Human Relations*, 7, 117-140.

Fraser-Thomas, J. L., Cote, J. & Deakin, J. (2005). Youth sport programs: An avenue to foster positive youth development. *Physical Education and Sport Pedagogy*, 10(1), 19-40.

Gardner, R. E. & Janelle, C. M. (2002) Legitimacy judgments of perceived aggression and assertion by contact and non-contact sport participants. *International journal of sport psychology*, 33, 290–306.

8 May 2014

⇨ The above information is reprinted with kind permission from Empower2Perform. Please visit www.empower2perform. com for further information.

Cricketers go back to school to teach the right spirit

Children around the country celebrated the end of term last week with some special cricketing visitors. Former Yorkshire captain and England cricketer Anthony McGrath surprised children in Newhall Primary School, Bradford with a special visit and Gloucestershire cricketer Ian Saxelby popped into Coniston Primary School near Bristol.

During the visit, both Ian and Anthony took part in MCC Spirit of Cricket Assemblies with the children. Using a video-based MCC Spirit of Cricket Assembly, created as part of a partnership with Chance to Shine, children discussed the meaning of 'rivalry'. The children learnt about respecting opposition, team-mates and officials, whilst being encouraged to play hard but fair.

After the assembly in Bradford, children took to the school playground for a coaching session, followed by a game with Anthony McGrath. Anthony touched on all aspects of the game during the coaching clinic, including bowling, batting and fielding.

Summing up his visit Ian said, 'It's been great. The kids got really involved and always wanted to put their hands up during the assembly, which is brilliant. It shows that kids do get involved with the game, a few lads here play cricket and it's brilliant for the area.

'Cricket is a great game as people become captains and leaders, learn teamwork and the discipline of training day in day out. There are plenty of life skills to be learnt around people playing sport.'

In 2013, around 400,000 children in 4,000 'Chance to Shine' schools will be introduced to the key MCC Spirit of Cricket messages enshrined in the Laws of the game, as a result of the MCC/Chance to Shine partnership. This will be done by communicating the MCC Spirit of Cricket message to children within schools through the special assemblies and organising intra school competitions.

⇨ The above information is reprinted with kind permission from Chance to Shine. Please visit www.chancetoshine.org for further information.

Top athletes give back over 4,000 days to community sport

UK Sport reveals how 2012 Olympic and Paralympic sports stars are helping to inspire a generation.

Athletes from the London 2012 Olympic and Paralympic Games have made thousands of appearances in schools and communities to help inspire a generation through sport, Culture Secretary Maria Miller announced today.

The UK Sport review which looks at what GB Olympic and Paralympic Athletes have done since London 2012 also reveals:

⇨ Of the 172 London 2012 medallists who reported back it is estimated that 77% have made at least one school or community appearance

⇨ 45% of these London 2012 medallists have already made five or more visits

⇨ Ten sports have averaged five appearances or more per athlete.

In August, Prime Minister David Cameron announced continued government funding for elite sport beyond the lifetime of the current Parliament and asked all funded athletes to give up to five days a year to inspire children and young people to get involved in sport.

This decision allowed UK Sport to invest a record £355 million of National Lottery and government funds for 44 sports to prepare for Rio 2016 and build on the incredible success of London 2012.

Culture Secretary Maria Miller today met with Olympic canoeing gold medallist Etienne Stott at Loughborough University's high-performance sports centre to hear about his experiences going into schools and community sport clubs.

Maria Miller said:

'We said that we would inspire a generation from London 2012 and these visits happening up and down the country help do exactly that. Our athletes are excellent role models and are making a great contribution to the Olympic and Paralympic legacy.'

23 July 2013

⇨ The above information is reprinted with kind permission from Department for Culture, Media & Sport and UK Sport. Please visit www.gov.uk for further information.

An analysis of the working conditions of professional sports players

An analysis of the working conditions of professional players of basketball, hockey, handball and rugby across a number of European member states.

Executive summary

The study examined the working conditions of professional sports players of ice hockey, rugby, handball and basketball. The findings raise a number of interesting issues about life in professional sports, the way players are treated, their attitudes to their career after sport; their health, their financial provisions and how these sports are organised in various European member states. What follows below is a snapshot of the key issues raised by professional players about their working life, which ought to serve as an action plan for the representatives of players, their clubs and the leagues in which they work.

Players without a contract

Although the majority of players in the study have a formal contract with their club, there are still many who do not, raising issues such as security of employment and the application of employment legislation to protect their rights at work.

Late payment of wages

In a number of countries, regardless of the type of sport, many players complained about receiving their wages late each month. In too many cases players state that their wages are sometimes or always paid late and this is something that ought to be addressed.

Lack of pension provisions

Many professional players have no pension, which raises doubts about individual players' capacity to make adequate provisions for retirement. UNI Europa Sport, employers and player associations all must work to raise the awareness among young players of the importance of having a pension.

Deficit of support from employers for education

While the evidence shows that sports players undertake some form of study while working as a professional, it is clear that players are not aware of educational opportunities for life beyond their career in sport. Furthermore, where players wish to participate in non-sport-related training, too often their employer is unwilling to support them to prepare for a new career after they retire from sport. This lack of support by employers could threaten the sustainability of professional sports as younger players become reluctant to pursue this occupation due to the difficulties posed by beginning a new career once they retire from sport.

Sport poses a high risk to health

The findings for all four sports in this study show that 63.2 per cent of sports players within the scope of the research feel that their professional sport poses a risk to their health. The responses from players across all four sports are littered with injuries – from broken bones, torn ligaments, concussion, injuries to the back and shoulders, damage to teeth, to stress, general fatigue and sleeping problems.

Low incidence of insurance against career-ending injuries

Given the high number of days sports players are absent from work due to injury, it is surprising that less than a third of all players in

the survey have a current insurance policy to protect them against a career-ending injury (31.4%), suggesting there is a significant amount of work to carry out by the stakeholders to ensure this issue is addressed.

Satisfaction with therapeutic support

Injured players rely upon the therapeutic support provided by their team's doctors and therapists; however, there are significant variations in the quality of support provided to injured players by their employer and these issue needs addressing.

Low quality of refereeing

One consistent complaint raised by players across all four sports was the apparent low quality of refereeing. The report contains suggestions for areas of improvement from players.

Overwhelming support for sector-wide collective agreement

Without doubt, the extent of support for the creation of an industry-wide collective agreement to regulate minimum standards for working time, wages, pension provisions and minimum insurance provisions was overwhelming among players from all countries and sports.

High incidence of harassment and discrimination

The degree to which players have individually been subjected to acts of intimidation, bullying, harassment and discrimination were highlighted in the survey. The findings show that in all sports and across all countries professional players have been exposed to various unwanted physical acts, threats and bullying and discrimination on the grounds of ethnicity and age.

Doping away from the workplace is considered an invasion of privacy

Players who have experienced being tested outside of their workplace are far more likely to consider this to constitute an invasion of their privacy than those who have not. The issue of privacy and testing therefore needs the attention of the European Commission and the social partners, to provide a methodology that ensures that players who do artificially enhance their performance in this way are caught, yet the process for doing so must rest within the boundaries of what is socially acceptable and must be designed with the issue of privacy at the centre.

Increase in evening work

Although the research findings for the prevalence of Sunday work show similar trends to those in the previous study, there does appear to be an increase in the number of handball players working in the evenings in both Spain and France.

Insufficient notice for changes to work schedule

Notice of changes to a player's work schedule are often inadequate and the vast majority of players in all countries and sports examined regularly experience changes to their work schedule, many through notice measured in hours not days.

Good work/life balance

The majority of players are satisfied that their working life fits in well with their wider commitments outside the workplace. Although, many players would prefer less matches in the season and more time off around the Christmas/New Year period.

Low awareness of disciplinary rules

A significant number of players are not familiar with their league or club's disciplinary rules, and those that are have not usually been sent a copy of the relevant documents by their employer.

Fines for misconduct

Players are often fined by their club as a disciplinary measure. While the value of the fine varies, many players often agree the level of their fine with their club. However, there do not appear to be any consistencies of this type of approach across specific sports or countries.

It is clear from the research that the perception of professional sports players among the general public is far from the reality of the majority of professional players. The research raises serious weaknesses in the regulation of employment in the sector and the negative effects this has on the working lives of professional players.

While these issues are not insurmountable and, in some cases, relatively simple actions would deliver significant improvements to the lives of players, improvements of the kind required will require a multilateral approach, involving the European Commission and its institutions, player associations, employers and the bodies regulating the leagues of each sport across all member states.

In addition, the absence of a social dialogue infrastructure within the sector presents a significant challenge to the stakeholders and therefore the role and influence of the European institutions will need to be maximised in order to create an awareness of the problems identified by the research, to bring employers into discussions with player associations and to create a framework for jointly constructed solutions.

Thus, improving the working lives of professional sports players will only be possible with the commitment and support of the European Commission in the coming months.

The necessary changes are feasible, but they require the commitment and full participation of the stakeholders and a genuine will on behalf of the European Commission.

2013

⇨ The above information is reprinted with kind permission from EU ATHLETES. Please visit www.euathletes.org for further information.

Are top athletes born or made?

By Mauro van de Looij, Sports & Achievement Psychologist and Child Psychologist

Have you ever seen the television series *Made* (MTV)? On this show one person wants to change his or her life and often wants to be 'made' the person of his or her dreams. Remember the girls wanting to be made popstars and the guys sport jocks? Whether you liked the show or not, it was a great format to help people become what they wanted to be. Now, let me ask you a question: do you think it is possible to be made in accordance with your dreams? Do you think top athletes are born or made?

More often than not you hear people credit quality to talent. For example, a football commentator may enthusiastically shout out loud: 'What a goal! This kid is amazingly talented!' Exactly what does talented mean? Does the commentator mean the player has incredible innate abilities which make him such a good striker? I reckon he does. Is he, then, right about attributing this player's quality to born characteristics? I believe he is not. Honestly, I reckon him – and his colleagues – to be way off with such an attribution.

Allow me to clarify myself on this one. First of all I believe your quality as a top athlete to consist of three aspects: innate abilities (talent), ability + motivation to learn and practice time. Innate abilities are of course the gifts you got from your parents (height for example). Ability + motivation to learn are necessary for developing, without it you will not develop (your talent). Practice time is the amount of time spent practising, the more time you spend the higher your quality will be.

Secondly there is a lot of research that has found effort, practice and learning to be more important than talent (e.g. Jowett, & Spray, 2013). In order to make my belief more credible I will discuss two examples that perfectly endorse my view that it takes more, a lot more, than sole talent to become an athlete of world-class status. I bring to you Cristiano Ronaldo and Lionel Messi – considered by many the best football players on the planet at this very moment. A lot of people speak about their giftedness and talent for football. Is that truly all it took them to become world class on the pitch? For my master's research (about Growth Mindset and Goal Orientations in Football) I took a look in their history and development. As it turns out, both Ronaldo and Messi have walked a similar path to become the quality players we know now. Heads up: it took them more than just talent!

When they were young they both enjoyed football greatly and had a very strong desire to become a professional football player. Therefore they have been playing football a lot during their younger years starting from around the age of five. At about 12 years of age, Ronaldo and Messi left their families for a place in a European Youth Football Academy (Ronaldo – Sporting Lisbon, Messi – FC Barcelona). Besides the shared dream they are also characterized for (and still have) their discipline to make the football dream come true. As opposed to loads of young boys who share the same dream, Ronaldo and Messi showed the discipline necessary in making this dream reality. The discipline consists of training, practising and learning. Throughout the teenage years they cared about and were busy with only one thing: the ball.

Were Messi and Ronaldo nothing special when they were young then? Of course they possessed qualities at a young age, otherwise they would not have been given the chance at a European Youth Football Academy. How did they develop then? According to youth coaches, Messi had something special at a young age, though he had a growth hormone deficit meaning he was delayed in his growth. Within FC Barcelona, controversy existed about Messi and his opportunity to become a professional football player. Eventually they took chances and were the only club willing and able to pay for the medical bills. Messi was offered the opportunity to make his dream come true at La Masia. To make it clear: even at that stage FC Barcelona were all but certain whether Messi could reach the professional football level. Imagine for a second that FC Barcelona had not given Messi that chance, we

probably would have never heard of him because he would not have had the opportunity to develop and improve his qualities (and deal with his medical setback). So Messi had to come a long way. Ronaldo stated his mum could have never guessed him to become such a great football player when he was young. This means it has never been a fact that Ronaldo would become one based upon his talent. For both Messi and Ronaldo nobody knew for sure they would be a professional football player in the future. Then what has been the key for Messi and Ronaldo? Practice! According to Ericsson (2006) – who is a psychologist – we need 10,000 hours of deliberate practice to become an expert in that field. If you have a dream, make sure you will reach that amount of hours to make it become reality. Now taking this into account, I reckon Ronaldo and Messi have passed this amount of hours easily by now and may even have by their early twenties. Could that be a reason for them winning the Ballon d'Or (Ronaldo – 2008, Messi – 2009, 2010, 2011, 2012)?

According to former team-mates, Ronaldo was always the first and the last person on the training ground. Goalkeeper van der Sar: 'After training he was always practising his free kick. If he needed a goalkeeper, to him I was the only option. If I asked him whether another goalkeeper could defend the goal during his free kick training he replied: "I only want to train with the best so I can become the best." Now that got me motivated alright.' Former manager Sir Alex Ferguson: 'Ronaldo's discipline was fantastic. I always saw him to be first and last on the pitch. Besides, he wouldn't give 100%, he gave 120%! Every time again.' Ruud van Nistelrooij who played alongside Ronaldo up front at Man United says: 'He is so complete. He trained and still trains every aspect of the game to become the best he can be. Heading, free kicks, two footedness, corner kicks, everything he practises. He is always training.' Team-mate Gerard Pique at FC Barcelona

about Lionel Messi: 'Aside from all the talent he's got, it's true that Messi learnt a lot at Barcelona. I don't know if Messi would be what he is today if he had left the club.'

Well, what has been key in becoming world-class players for Ronaldo and Messi? Practice, right! And let me ask you again, do you believe top athletes are born or made? I reckon you will say it is possible to be made a top athlete. Then why, you might ask, do 'we' attribute quality to talent? How come the commentator shouts out 'what an amazing talented player'? Good question!

The answer, I think, lies in the so-called fundamental attribution error-phenomenon. Did you ever go for lunch and experience the waiter or waitress to be unfriendly to you? What attribution did or would you make for this waiter's odd behaviour? Probably you say this waiter is not a nice guy at all, he might even be a schmuck and not fit for the job like the way he is (not) serving you. This attribution is perfectly understandable as our minds have not got the time, energy or interest to take all circumstances that could influence someone's behaviour into account. However, maybe the waiter had a bad day – he got dumped by his girlfriend, he failed for his driving licence or has been bothered by other customers all day long – and consequently could not be friendly to you. If you think about such a scenario then can you understand the waiter's behaviour (better)? In essence the waiter's example is exactly what 'we' do regarding athletes. We forget to look to the history and development of top athletes. Don't get me wrong, I understand attributing behaviour (quality on the pitch) to the person (talent) perfectly, but to say the very least it hardly ever is the correct attribution to make.

Therefore, try to take circumstances into account, for you may be less frustrated. As for sports, imagine young children playing a nice game of football. If they believe talent is all it takes to become a professional football player, your chances of becoming one are less than 1%

or so, for there's always a person out there who's more talented than you are. Therefore you might lose interest, don't try as hard as you could and may even quit playing. Now, if we all start believing and expressing it took the likes of Ronaldo, Messi, Federer, Nadal and Tiger Woods many hours of practice, effort and learning to become such great athletes, maybe our kids will learn to appreciate the value of working hard. Maybe they will add the discipline necessary for their dream to come true. And what is more beautiful than our dreams coming true?

I would like to conclude by stating top athletes are made and never born. However, if you happen to find a baby doing all the tricks our top athletes do nowadays, I am more than interested in hearing more about this little genius. To underline that it takes effort more than talent, I have to confess I have rewritten this article a few times before it went public for you to read. To me, practice does make perfect!

References

⇨ Jowett, N. & Spray, C.M. (2013). British Olympic Hopefuls: The antecedents and consequences of implicit ability beliefs in elite track and field athletes. *Psychology of Sport and Exercise*, 14, 145–153.

⇨ CNN Documentary about Cristiano Ronaldo – http://www.youtube.com/watch?v=iHkHTpuGaD8.

⇨ ITV Documentary about Lionel Messi – http://www.dailymotion.com/video/xpas6i_messi-belgeseli-ingilizce_sport.

6 December 2013

Inclusion

Chapter 2

Post-Games evaluation: disability

The Games improved attitudes to disability and provided new opportunities for disabled people to participate in society.

The 2012 Olympic and Paralympic Games were a unique opportunity for sharing positive messages about disabled people, which led to an upswell in positive public attitudes and perceptions of disabled people.

The clearest example of this opportunity for positive images about disabled people is the scale of coverage and support for the Paralympic Games. Channel 4 provided unprecedented levels of television and multi-media coverage of the Paralympics designed to challenge perceptions of disabled people. More than 500 hours of coverage were broadcast across all platforms, 350 hours over the stated target and four times more than from the Beijing Paralympics in 2008. It included 16 hours of live coverage every day and 1.3 million live streams online. The coverage reached an unprecedented share of the audience, and achieved record viewing figures. Almost 40 million people – more than two thirds of the UK population – viewed the Paralympic Games on TV.[1] Overall, 25% of all TV viewers watched Channel 4's coverage every day. Peak viewing levels reached 11.6 million for the opening ceremony – Channel 4's biggest audience in more than a decade – and 6.3 million watched Jonnie Peacock win Gold in the T44 100 m, the largest rating for a single Paralympic event. Channel 4 also ensured that 50% of on-screen talent for Paralympic broadcasts were disabled people.

'Almost 40 million people – more than two thirds of the UK population – viewed the Paralympic Games on TV'

Other activities took place that complemented this work to improve public attitudes, including work in schools on disability sports through the Get Set programme, volunteering opportunities offered by the Games Maker scheme and the Unlimited programme of arts and cultural activities for disabled people as part of the Cultural Olympiad. Additionally, on London's South Bank a raft of accessibility improvements formed part of the Government's flagship public realm improvements.

Research to explore the impact of these activities has shown generally positive attitudes towards the Paralympics and its potential to reduce prejudice. Just under a quarter of respondents to the British Social Attitudes Survey felt that the Paralympic Games would reduce prejudice 'a lot', and almost 40% felt it would reduce prejudice 'a little'. This figure was significantly higher for those responding in the post-Games period, indicating that the success of the event itself reinforced this view. However, despite this stated positive perception of the Games, overarching measures of attitudes towards disabled people have yet to show a notable improvement.

'...by March 2013 a quarter of people were still saying that the Paralympic Games caused them to have a 'much more positive view' of disabled people'

Other pieces of research also showed positive changes in attitudes after the Paralympics. Research by the disability charity Scope found that 62% of disabled people believed the Paralympics could improve attitudes towards disabled people. Independent media analysis showed a major improvement in the way disability was covered in the press in the year of the Paralympics, with a peak in the level of coverage of disabled people which used positive and empowering terminology.

How long the uplift in public attitudes will last is more questionable. Stakeholders broadly agreed that the improvement in attitudes was at risk of being a relatively short-term improvement and that developments and press coverage since the end of the Games, especially in early 2013 around the context of benefit reform, had affected public perceptions. Encouragingly, rolling survey evidence still being collected[2] shows that even by March 2013 a quarter of people were still saying that the Paralympic Games caused them to have a 'much more positive view' of disabled people. One stakeholder noted that:

'For us what this shows is that the Paralympics were a breakthrough moment. But it takes longer than a fortnight to change attitudes. We should be asking what we can do to build on it and keep it going.'

'Participation in sport and recreational activity by disabled people also increased by 4.2 percentage points in 2012 from 2005/06'

The Games also opened up a range of volunteering, cultural and sporting opportunities for disabled people that did not exist before. Participation in volunteering by disabled people increased year-on-year to 2012, compared to 2005/06, and 4% of Games Maker volunteers had a disability. There was also an increase in engagement in arts and cultural activity by those with a disability in 2012, helping to narrow the gap with participation levels amongst non-disabled people. The level of involvement of disabled artists in the cultural programme was unprecedented and contributed to a greater credibility of the disability arts sector and the opportunity to showcase art to the mainstream arts sector.

Participation in sport and recreational activity[3] by disabled people also increased by 4.2 percentage points in 2012 from 2005/06. This was in part driven by legacy programmes such as the Inclusive Sport Fund, which is investing over £10 million of National Lottery funding into projects designed to increase the number of disabled young people and adults regularly playing sport, along with opportunities offered by the School Games, Sportivate, Inspire projects and Legacy Trust UK. The School Games national event in May 2012 in the Olympic Park involved 167 disabled athletes (11.6% of the total) and all the facilities in the Olympic Park have been designed to be accessible to disabled participants and attendees.

Collectively, these developments – as a result of the Games – provided an opportunity for change that would not have been possible on an equivalent scale and would not have happened otherwise. Whether improvements in attitudes to disabled people are lasting will take longer to understand but the initial evidence is positive.

54% of adults without an impairment said they experienced at least one barrier to playing sport compared to **72% of adults with an impairment**

Source: Annual Report 2011-2012,

Footnotes

1. Channel 4 (2012) The London 2012 Games. Brought to you by Channel 4. Based on three minute reach of TV coverage over duration of the Paralympic Games

2. Games-related questions commissioned by Department for Work and Pensions were asked in five waves of the Office for National Statistics (ONS) Opinions and Lifestyle Survey from November 2012 to March 2013.

3. Based on one x 30 minutes of moderate intensity sport in the last week including recreational cycling and walking as measured by Taking Part.

July 2013

⇨ The above information is reprinted with kind permission from the Department for Culture, Media & Sport. Please visit www.gov.uk for further information.

Boost for disability sport

One of the guiding principles of the Olympics is the importance of participation as opposed to winning.

'The essential thing is not to have conquered but to have fought well,' said the father of the modern Olympic movement, Baron Pierre de Coubertin.

Paralympians are living examples of people who have triumphed over adversity and 'fought well'.

Every Paralympian has an inspirational story to tell. Most people would be impressed and inspired by the sight of an athlete with missing limbs sprinting faster than most able-bodied people.

Read inspiring stories from Paralympians:

⇨ David Weir

⇨ Sarah Storey

⇨ Ian Rose

⇨ David Roberts.

The British Paralympic Association (BPA) hopes that the London 2012 Games will continue to inspire disabled people of all ages to take up sport, either competitively or for its health benefits.

The BPA's Parasport website aims to increase participation in disability sport by directing people to suitable sports, opportunities, clubs and facilities in their area.

The Parasport website is designed to improve access to regional sports facilities for disabled people.

'Many young people do not know how to access sport for the disabled in their local area,' said a Parasport spokesman. 'Equally, we needed to find new athletes for the GB team in time for 2012 and beyond. We hope this scheme helps to extend the talent pool.'

Britain's got talent

Britain has one of the best records at the Paralympic Games, which were first held in 1960 in Rome. The BPA wants Britain to continue to set the standards in disability sport internationally and to nurture new talent.

The Parasport website is the first of its kind in the UK. Its goal is to inspire anyone with a disability to lead an active lifestyle and enjoy the benefits of participating in sport, such as health, inclusion and social development.

The website has a number of features, including a self-assessment wizard, which allows the user to enter their disability and find suitable sports to participate in. There is information on all the different parasports, videos, photographs and regular news updates.

While the Paralympic sports are at the forefront of disability sporting opportunities, there are plenty of non-Paralympic sports available too. The disability world has a wide variety of sports, including zone hockey, transplant sports, water-skiing, angling, wheelchair dance, hand cycling, motor sports, inclusive gyms and much more.

With its growing clubs and events database, the Parasport website will support and develop as many of these sporting opportunities as possible.

Baroness Tanni Grey-Thompson, Britain's most successful wheelchair athlete, believes the Parasport website will increase the opportunities available to disabled people throughout the UK.

'We want to encourage more youngsters, as well as the disabled community as a whole, to take up sport either competitively or for health reasons,' she says.

1 July 2013

⇨ The above information is reprinted with kind permission from NHS Choices. Please visit www.nhs.uk for further information.

Too many foreign signings, say football fans

By Chris Polechonski

This week Arsenal midfielder Jack Wilshere made comments in which he stated that 'the only people who should play for England are English people'. This was followed today by a new 'State of the Game' study from the BBC, showing that English footballers play less than one third of all the minutes in the Premier League.

New YouGov research, carried out following the closure of the most recent transfer window, reveals that more than three quarters of football fans (78%) think Premier League clubs are signing too many foreign players. Only 6% disagree.

Similarly, nearly four in five fans (79%) believe there should be a limit on the number of foreign players a Premier League team has in their match-day squad, while about one in six (16%) say there should not be a cap.

The research suggests football fans agree with previous concerns expressed by FA Chairman, Greg Dyke, about the impact overseas players are having in the top flight on the national game.

10 October 2013

⇨ The above information is reprinted with kind permission from YouGov. Please visit www.yougov.co.uk for further information.

Racism in football exists – but do fans think it's a problem?

91% of football fans in England think racism exists in football – the second highest in Europe – but they are amongst least likely to say it is a serious problem.

By Luke Chambers

YouGov interviewed fans and the general public in England, Scotland, France, Germany, Spain, Italy and The Netherlands about their attitudes to racism and homophobia in football.

Reports from fans across Europe consistently show that racism exists in football. Italian football tops the league, with 92% of fans saying it exists in Italian football. England is a close second with 91%, with Spanish fans reporting the lowest incidence of racism, with 73% feeling that it exists.

Of those who say that racism exists, English fans are amongst the least likely to view the problem as serious (43%). Scottish fans are the least likely to see racism as a serious problem (38%), with Italian fans the most likely (71%).

The issue has recently come to prominence in Italian football. In January, former AC Milan forward Kevin-Prince Boateng became the first player to walk off the pitch in response to racist chanting, with the game later abandoned. Since then a referee has stopped a match between AC Milan and Roma in response to the problem, and Lazio were forced to close a stand of their stadium for the opening weekend of the Italian season following persistent problems.

English fans give clubs and players the most credit for combating racism, with 40% feeling that they are doing enough. Despite this, every football authority put to English fans was judged to not be doing enough to combat racism. Just 17% of English fans feel that international authorities such as FIFA and UEFA are doing enough.

Across Europe, football fans feel that players, clubs, national and international governing bodies and fans themselves are not doing enough to combat the problem. On average across the seven countries surveyed, only 22% of fans feel that the international bodies such as UEFA and FIFA are doing enough to tackle racism.

FIFA President Sepp Blatter caused controversy in 2011 by suggesting race-related incidents could be settled with a post-match handshake; meanwhile Head of UEFA Michel Platini stated any player walking off the pitch at Euro 2016 because of racist chanting would be booked.

16 September 2013

⇨ The above information is reprinted with kind permission from YouGov. Please visit www.yougov.co.uk for further information.

Out in Sport

LGBT students' experiences of sport.

Executive summary

For many students, including many lesbian, gay, bisexual and trans (LGBT) students who participated in this research, sport is an important part of university or college life. Yet many LGBT students feel excluded or uncomfortable participating in sport because of factors including the culture, structure and physical environment in which sport takes place.

In 2011, as the UK prepared to host one of the biggest sporting events in the world, the NUS LGBT campaign launched a research project into the sporting experiences of LGBT students. The project consisted of a literature review, an online survey of 845 LGBT students and nine workshops with students across the UK. Both the survey and the workshops explored LGBT students' experiences participating in and coming out in sport, as well as the barriers that prevent LGBT students from getting more involved in sport.

The NUS LGBT campaign believes that LGBT students should be able to fully enjoy and benefit from participation in sport. This report makes specific recommendations for sports teams, students' unions, institutions and other organisations to enable them to work towards achieving this goal.

Participation in sport

The majority of LGBT students participate in sport or fitness activities of some type, although the type of sport and activity varies across sexual orientation and gender identity.

⇨ 59.1 per cent of LGBT students participate in an individual sport or fitness activity, 34.6 per cent participate in an organised team sport and 23.0 per cent participate in an informal team sport. Lesbian women are much more likely than any other group to participate in an organised team sport, with 52.0 per cent of respondents doing so.

⇨ Running is the most common form of sporting activity overall, with 18.8 per cent of respondents participating. Going to the gym is more popular with gay and bisexual men, while rugby is more popular with lesbian women.

⇨ Most LGBT students are participating in sport organised by their students' union (50.9 per cent) or their university/college (27.1 per cent).

Experiences in sport

Many LGBT students who participate in sport have a positive experience while doing so.

⇨ Nearly two thirds (62.2 per cent) of LGBT students who participate in team sport are open about their sexual orientation or gender identity to their team-mates and coaches.

⇨ 17.1 per cent of LGBT students who participate in team sport are not open to anyone. The main reason for this was that they do not think it is relevant, but 20.5 per cent of those who are not out are worried it might result in verbal or physical abuse on account of homophobia, transphobia or biphobia.

⇨ Only about a third of LGBT students (36.6 per cent) agreed or strongly agreed that equality policies with regards to sport were visible at their institution.

Barriers to participation

Although many LGBT students who do not participate in sport are simply not interested or do not have the time, the research has identified that there are clear cultural, structural and physical barriers that prevent some LGBT students from participating in sport.

⇨ 46.8 per cent of LGBT students who do not participate in sport find the culture around sport alienating or unwelcoming.

⇨ 41.9 per cent had a negative experience at school which has meant that they don't want to get involved at college or university.

⇨ 14.3 per cent had experienced homophobia, biphobia, or transphobia which has put them off from participating.

⇨ 18.7 per cent were put off by gendered sports teams and this rose to 38.9 per cent of trans respondents.

⇨ 9.4 per cent were put off by gender-specific kit and/or clothing and this rose to 36.1 per cent for trans respondents.

⇨ 12.8 per cent do not find the facilities, such as showers or changing rooms, inclusive and this rose to 36.1 per cent for trans respondents.

Making sport more inclusive

LGBT students have clear opinions on the way that sport can be made more inclusive.

⇨ The most popular suggestion for encouraging more LGBT people to be involved in sport was tackling homophobia/transphobia/biphobia in sport within schools, which received the support of 48.3 per cent of LGBT students.

⇨ There was also substantial support for celebrating LGBT role models in sport; training for staff and coaches; training for sports societies; a clear and visible equality policy; having more mixed-gender sports teams; and ensuring facilities are gender neutral.

Recommendations

For sports teams and societies

Sports teams and societies and others who are directly involved in the delivery of sporting experiences for students should:

⇨ **Publicise LGBT-friendliness**: In order to create an environment that is welcoming to LGBT students, sports teams and societies should publicly demonstrate their inclusiveness, such as through the Government's charter for action on tackling homophobia, biphobia and transphobia in sport.

⇨ **Adopt a zero tolerance to homophobia policy**: Sports teams and societies need to be clear that homophobic, biphobic and transphobic abuse is unacceptable through a clearly articulated zero tolerance policy. This will help to ensure that LGBT students feel safe to participate in sport.

⇨ **Provide guidance for trans students**: Sports teams and societies should make available a clear and easily accessible policy on whether and under what conditions, trans students are eligible to participate and/or compete in sport.

For students' unions

Students' unions, providers of further and higher education, national governing bodies of sport, and others who provide and regulate sport for students should:

⇨ **Provide more mixed-gender sporting options**: Students' unions and others that provide and regulate sport should make more mixed-gender teams available in order to mitigate the effects of gender stereotypes in sport and enable LGBT students to feel more comfortable participating.

⇨ **Audit sports facilities**: Students should have the option of single-cubicle, gender-neutral facilities such as showers and changing rooms. Educational institutions and others providing sports facilities should audit their existing facilities to assess how inclusive they are and include LGBT students in this process.

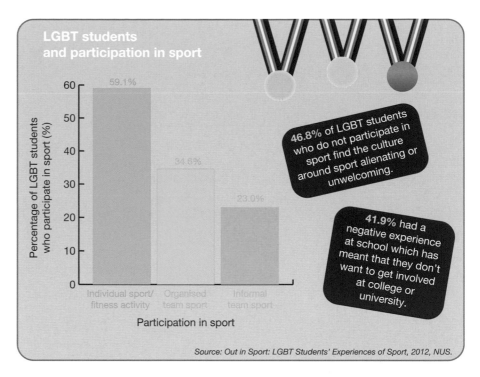

Source: Out in Sport: LGBT Students' Experiences of Sport, 2012, NUS.

46.8% of LGBT students who do not participate in sport find the culture around sport alienating or unwelcoming.

41.9% had a negative experience at school which has meant that they don't want to get involved at college or university.

New facilities should be built with the express purpose of being inclusive to all.

⇨ **Train sports teams and societies**: Students' unions and others organising the provision of sport should provide training that enables sports teams and societies to create a welcoming, supportive environment where LGBT students feel comfortable being open about their sexual orientation or gender identity and empowers them to eliminate homophobia, transphobia and biphobia from sport.

⇨ **Train coaches and other sports staff**: Organisations that provide and regulate sport should provide training for coaches and staff on how to lead LGBT-positive environments. Organisations involved in the training of coaches should incorporate LGBT issues into their training provision.

⇨ **Support and celebrate LGBT role models**: Only athletes themselves can decide whether to be open about their sexuality, but organisations providing sporting opportunities should support those who do come out and celebrate them as role models, whether on a national or local level. Organisations should strive to create an atmosphere in

which athletes are comfortable and supported in being open about their sexuality.

For schools

Schools and other providers of sports activities for under-16-year-olds should:

⇨ **Teach LGBT-inclusiveness**: Schools and other providers of sports activities for under-16-year-olds should use sport as a way to teach children that homophobia, biphobia and transphobia are unacceptable and that all members of a sports team should contribute to creating an inclusive environment.

⇨ **Encourage a broad range of sporting activities**: Schools and other providers of sports activities should make an effort to support students to participate in a broad range of sports, including those that are not typical for their gender.

⇨ The above information is reprinted with kind permission from the National Union of Students (NUS). Please visit www.nus.org.uk for further information.

Transsexual people and competitive sport

The evidence from NGBs (National Governing Bodies) in the UK clearly suggests that there are a number of transsexual people seeking to play competitive sport and their age range, ability and ambition varies considerably. NGBs will need to have policies and procedures in place with regard to transsexual people playing competitive sport that reflects this range.

Examples of transsexual athletes in the public domain include:

⇨ Renee Richards who played women's tennis in the 1970s and who is believed to have been the first transsexual professional athlete.

⇨ Canadian Michelle Dumaresq who was Canada's downhill mountain bike champion in 2003 and competed on the pro circuit.

⇨ Nong Tum was a champion kickboxer in Thailand and the subject of the movie *Beautiful Boxer*. She won 22 professional fights, 18 by knockout, and is a household name in her home country. Officially retired in 1999 she made a comeback in 2006.

⇨ Mianne Bagger may be the best known transsexual in professional sport today. Since 2004 she has been a touring professional golfer competing on tours in Europe and Australia.

⇨ Keelin Godsey is an athlete competing in the hammer throw. He narrowly missed making the Olympic team. 'Up till now I have competed as a woman and was pre-everything. I am now currently taking Testosterone, started 8/7/12, and am navigating the world of sports, specifically track and field, as a transitioning athlete. I will be trying to make it as a male hammer thrower.'

'... it's only a matter of time before a transsexual athlete becomes the first to represent his or her country at the Olympics. That day will be one to celebrate as another part of a long tradition of overcoming barriers to competition.' Donna Rose.

Donna Rose is an author and educator and an elected member of the Human Rights Campaign Business Council. She is a male-to-female transsexual and an advocate and spokesperson for transgender people and issues.

Key issues for NGBs

Through feedback from NGBs we have identified some recurring concerns about how to approach the inclusion of transsexual people in competitive sport, these include:

⇨ Confusion about the terminology and a lack of confidence about what terms to use.

⇨ Lack of knowledge and understanding of equality legislation and the implications for NGBs including single-sex, mixed-sex competition and age-restricted competition.

⇨ Concerns about applying international competition regulations to domestic competition.

⇨ Perception that transsexual females will have an unfair advantage over other female competitors.

⇨ Concerns over the safety of competitors – particularly in close contact sport.

⇨ Lack of an identified central point of contact in the NGB who is confident and competent to manage issues with regard to transsexual people.

⇨ Local organisations, e.g. clubs and leagues, developing their own policies with regard to transsexual people playing competitive sport due to lack of clear guidance or communication from the NGB.

⇨ Managing people's attitudes, prejudices and stereotyping in sport about transsexual people.

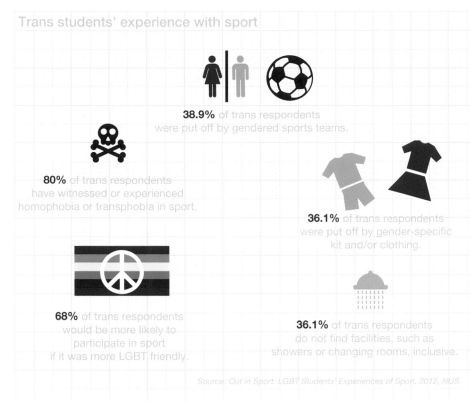

Trans students' experience with sport

38.9% of trans respondents were put off by gendered sports teams.

80% of trans respondents have witnessed or experienced homophobia or transphobia in sport.

36.1% of trans respondents were put off by gender-specific kit and/or clothing.

68% of trans respondents would be more likely to participate in sport if it was more LGBT friendly.

36.1% of trans respondents do not find facilities, such as showers or changing rooms, inclusive.

Source: Out in Sport: LGBT Students' Experiences of Sport, 2012, NUS.

An interview with a transsexual woman playing competitive hockey – February 2013

What were your reasons for getting involved in sport and hockey in particular?

I wanted to be part of something fun and accepted as just part of a larger team, while having the chance to build new friendships. It was refreshing to make new friends who were not aware of my birth gender; I was totally accepted.

I chose hockey because it's a team sport. You can't succeed at hockey as a lone player; you have to work part of together as a team, so the focus is on the team.

How have the people at the club supported you?

Everyone has been amazing, much better than I imagined. I've started to make new friendships and I'm totally accepted as one of the girls. I've only discussed my circumstances with a small group and they have treated me with respect and maintained confidentiality.

When I started playing competitively it was really good to have a mentor from my club who I could turn to and ask any awkward questions and discuss any challenges like locker rooms, showers and parents, or what if someone challenged me or objected, etc. The best support I have had is to be treated the same as everyone else, and that's all I want.

What were the barriers to you getting involved?

I was terrified to go along although I've wanted to play for ages. I was simply too afraid of rejection. One of the hardest parts about transitioning is social transition,

and it requires a lot of effort to re-build friendships and re-establish yourself in a new role while dealing with your history.

Now you are starting to play competitively how do you feel, are you enjoying it, what benefits are you finding for yourself?

I have something to look forward to every week and I'm gaining much more confidence with who I am as a person while making new friendships.

Simply being accepted as female and part of a team really builds my confidence both at work and socially. I've also started running and have entered a half-marathon charity race.

What would have made your experience of joining a club easier?

When I started hockey training I wasn't initially allowed to participate in competitions and this was really hard as it set me apart from everyone else. However, since the EHB policy changes it will be much easier for other transgender men and women who want to play. Hopefully other sports will adopt a similar approach.

I think it's particularly hard for transgender women to play sport. As a transgender woman you need to overcome a lot of fear and lack of confidence and having no prior sporting experience or reference, it was hard. But the way I saw it is that many women lack confidence and have many insecurities, and in this respect I'm just the same as everyone else.

The hardest part was the first few weeks. Turning up to hockey training when there was 50 other women who all seemed to know each other really well was very intimidating, especially as I'd never even held a hockey stick before; I had to start with the basics 'this is the end you hold'.

What would you say to another transsexual female who is thinking about playing competitive sport?

I would just say, 'Give it a go! It's really good fun, you will make friends and get really fit too.'

9 January 2014

⇨ The above information is reprinted with kind permission from Sport Northern Ireland. Please visit www.sportni.net for further information.

© Sport Northern Ireland 2014

Women in sport

By Hetty Knox

SportWatch

SportWatch are a Bristol-based organisation dedicated to providing increased coverage of women's sport in Bristol. Their website is regularly updated to promote upcoming sporting events in Bristol and feature regular stories on local women athletes, as well as commentary, sports reports, and news articles. The campaign is only two months old and is part of the local Bristol Fawcett group that campaigns for gender equality and women's rights in Bristol. They gave evidence to the recent Mayor's Sport Commission which aims to raise sporting aspirations in the city. We spoke to the founders of SportWatch.

What were the reasons for undertaking the campaign?

I came late to sport and really loved it, it made a massive difference to me personally in terms of I was going through a stressful job reaching the higher echelons of management but not really feeling I had all the skills, and sport really helped me with that. It helped me to deal with stress and was an outlet, and one of the really important things about not always getting it right, sport teaches you that as long as you try your hardest that's OK. So that's a big life lesson and to me it feels natural that if I feel passionate about something I will campaign for it. So to reflect on that I thought 'hang on a minute, why wasn't I playing sport since I was young?'

What evidence did you give to the mayor's commission?

We discussed the evidence of women participating less in sport. 12% of men participate in team sport a week and less than 2% of women do. We also talked about the benefits of sport that are unique to women and the wider society, benefits such as women

managers competing in sport and the way sport can help with leadership skills. We discussed the barriers in sport that are unique to women such as cultural barriers, and how girls aren't necessarily given the same encouragement at school and that doing sport is seen as unfeminine.

What was the response like to your evidence?

It was a little disappointing that it wasn't on their radar already, but they were really receptive and I do feel confident that our evidence will make a change. Everyone just immediately accepted that there is a problem. The mayor really wants Bristol to be a city of sport. People think that Bristol is rubbish at sport but what they really mean is that Bristol is rubbish at men's sport! So what we were trying to focus on is that we have lots of really great women's sport to build upon. We have number two football team, a Bristol ladies rugby team that plays in the premiership and three of their players play for England, and the Clifton ladies hockey team are at the top of their national league.

With the mayor wanting Bristol to be a sporting city, the problem is that we are not going to be able to attract the top men's international games because we don't have the facilities, but there might be opportunity to attract a big women's event. Also, when doing the analysis of the *Bristol Post* in October, there was no coverage of women's sport; I think that highlights the point of the male, dominated sports media industry.

Is it a money problem? A lot of women would go to fitness classes etc. but many of them say that they can't afford to go regularly.

I think it goes back to the culture that will root women to a fitness class rather than pick up a football and kick it about for free. I don't think perceptions of what is and isn't OK for your gender to do is formed at a really young age. I spoke to a teacher of seven- and eight-year-old girls and they didn't want to do sport because they didn't want to get sweaty or they don't see it as being girly or attractive. The image perception sets in at a really young

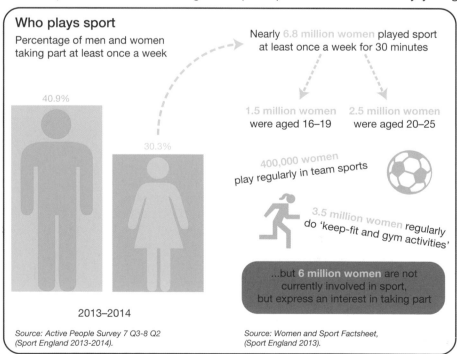

Who plays sport

Percentage of men and women taking part at least once a week

40.9%

30.3%

2013–2014

Source: Active People Survey 7 Q3-8 Q2 (Sport England 2013-2014).

Nearly 6.8 million women played sport at least once a week for 30 minutes

1.5 million women were aged 16–19

2.5 million women were aged 20–25

400,000 women play regularly in team sports

3.5 million women regularly do 'keep-fit and gym activities'

...but 6 million women are not currently involved in sport, but express an interest in taking part

Source: Women and Sport Factsheet, (Sport England 2013).

age. Research says that the women that always play sport have less body issues. Sport has the potential to help so many girls and women.

What do you think of the labels in sport? For example, there is football and then there is women's football.

We should make an effort to put the gender in front of the sport, for example men's rugby not just rugby. The other thought is that in an ideal world, one word would encompass both genders, such as athletics. We had a big debate over this for the name of the website, we deliberately called it SportWatch as it should be an inclusive term that doesn't exclude either gender.

What do you think of the lack of women on the boards of National Governing Bodies in sport?

If you don't have women at the table then people just aren't thinking about it, you've got to challenge that. In terms of getting more women coaching too, it can be quite inaccessible, costly and take a lot of time; if I was a woman with a family I probably wouldn't be able to do that. But I do think that if you don't have women in management and in the sporting bodies nobody is thinking that actually we should structure this differently.

How can we give more coverage to women's sport?

One of the reasons the media gives for not covering women's sport is because football is so popular, at the moment 50% of *The Guardian* coverage is football but if they did it on demand it would be 75%. So why don't we focus on the fact that we do have a really good women's football team because there is likely already a really big fan base there based on the fact that men's football is so popular. One of the reasons that men's football is popular is because it has that loyalty, and people really stick with their team and the politics that go with it. So we need to get this with the women's side and get people engaged.

If you would like to know more about SportWatch or get information

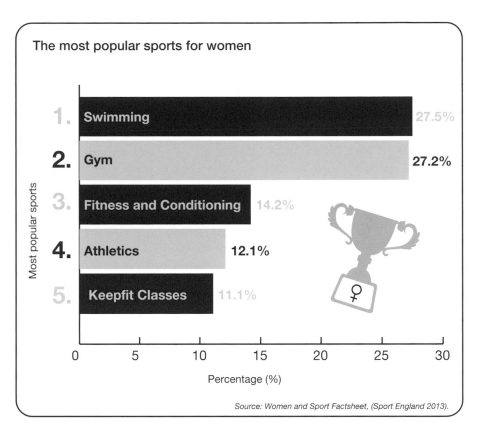

The most popular sports for women

1. Swimming — 27.5%
2. Gym — 27.2%
3. Fitness and Conditioning — 14.2%
4. Athletics — 12.1%
5. Keepfit Classes — 11.1%

Most popular sports (y-axis)
Percentage (%) (x-axis): 0, 5, 10, 15, 20, 25, 30

Source: Women and Sport Factsheet, (Sport England 2013).

about upcoming women's sport fixtures in Bristol, visit their website: http://sportwatchbristol. wordpress.com. Or if you would like to contribute to SportWatch Bristol they are keen to receive articles on the following: Reporting of local sporting events, interviews or features with women athletes and sports commentary, specifically in relation to women and girls

E-mail: sport@bristolfawcett.org.uk

Sportsister

Sportsister is a prominent voice in celebrating, inspiring and encouraging women's participation in sport at all levels. Founded in 2008, just before the Beijing Olympics, it is the leading women's sports magazine in the UK with approximately 30,000 readers per month. We spoke to the editor, Danielle Sellwood about the issues concerning women's sport

What was the drive for setting up Sportsister?

No one was talking about the issue back then (2008). For my job I spent a lot of time looking at gaps in the market in the sports industry, and the women's market in terms of clothing and products was booming but there was no media covering women's sport. Also, I was a sports woman myself, I was an international level canoeist, and it's always been something that's on my mind. I had a few experiences when I was canoeing and the press coverage was appalling. There was one particular occasion when I was doing the Devizes to Westminster race, I was in a good mixed crew – we were tipped to be in the top three overall. One of the newspapers got in touch as it was quite an interesting story, I asked the interviewer what the chances of us getting into the paper were as it would be great for canoeing to get a mention. She said, 'well you are blonde so as long as the pictures come out well there is a good chance'. I was completely staggered – canoeing for 125 miles and beating half the blokes wasn't enough, I had to look glamorous as well. The photographs didn't come out particularly well because I didn't bother to pose for them in that way, it was a training shot. We didn't get featured. I just thought that was ridiculous and something needed to be done. We have all seen a lot of women sports stars get overlooked. Chrissie Wellington is a prime example, she's famous within her sport and probably in other countries but the average person on the street wouldn't recognise her. She's an incredible athlete and deserves a much higher profile than she has.

Your website is quite tailored at the moment to the coverage of elite athletes; do you have any drive to focus on making sports more accessible for women?

When we set up *Sportsister* it was about rebranding sport for women and being like your sporty friend that showed you all about sport and how to get involved. Because women's sports stars are starting to get more coverage we are stepping away from the news slightly; although we will cover this, what we do want to do for 2014 is make sport much more about helping women get involved in sport. More about training plans etc. and we are going to go out to events and make our presence known. We have lots of exciting plans that are much more about recreational sport and participation.

Is the lack of media coverage that women in sport get due to the male domination of the sports media industry?

I'll give you an example of the first press day I went to, it was the pre-Olympic press day for cycling for the 2008 Beijing Olympics. There were about 100 people there including press and athletes – Rebecca Romero and Bradley Wiggins were there (before he was famous!) and I was the only female journalist. One of the other journalists asked me where the loo was because they just assumed that I must work in PR, I couldn't possibly be a journalist.

This is changing and has changed a lot in the past five years, but we've got a long way to catch up to have parity of women working within the sports industry. On one hand we've hardly got any women working in the sports industry (in journalism) and on the other, the vast majority of men that are working in the industry love the traditional sports. They might report now and then on the minority sports but they have no real interest

or love of them so it's not a natural thing for them to do. It's as much a problem for the minority sports as it is for women's sport. If we look at the Sport Personality of the Year Award contenders there are some really significant men not on that list, so it's not just about the women, it's about sport generally. When the Olympics are on everyone loves seeing them but as soon as it is all finished people forget that we loved hearing about canoeists or we loved the rowers or people from different sports. For some of them their achievements are arguably more impressive because they are not on huge grants, most of them are struggling and are having to make a much bigger commitment for their sport but the standard they are reaching is no less than the professional (well-paid) athletes. I think it is important for youngsters growing up to see lots of sports covered, I firmly believe that there is a sport for everybody but if you only ever see three of them in the papers and you don't like those then you might think that sport's not for you.

What do you think the other key issues are facing women in sport; do you think a lot of it is to do with education?

We need to get women being seen doing sport in all sorts of media, whether it is on TV, in magazines so it becomes a lot more normal, regardless of if they are elite or if it is just a local fun run – just being visible. So although obviously it

comes down to lots more coverage for elite stars, a lot of the magazines try to speak about grass roots programmes to make it seem more accessible. For young teenage girls, it obviously depends on the school and the teaching for them, it is more who they see on a daily basis. And mostly they are bombarded with celebrities and pop stars and we need to make sure that they are bombarded by positive role models that are female role models across all different sports who all have a different style, look or body shape. The problem sometimes is that they lump sportswomen into one type of person, one sort of look. But if you take an athlete from surfing and from mountain biking and a Jessica Ennis and a swimmer, they are all potentially very different characters and body shapes, and have different enjoyments of different sports. There is such a vast variety of sports out there and it is important that young girls are exposed to all those possibilities.

10 December 2013

⇨ The above information is reprinted with kind permission from Epigram. Please visit www.epigram.org.uk for further information.

Barriers to sports participation for women and girls

Participation in sport for women and girls is not as high as it could be. This is not only a health concern, but also a wider social and economic development issue.

Below is a list which shows the physical, personal and emotional barriers that women and girls face when it comes to participating in sport:

⇨ Lack of time and childcare

⇨ Lack of money

⇨ Personal safety

⇨ Funding

⇨ Access to facilities

⇨ Body image

⇨ Clothing and equipment

⇨ Lack of self-confidence

⇨ Parents and adult influence

⇨ Male-dominated culture of sport

⇨ Invisibility in media

⇨ Lack of role models

Source: Women and Sport Factsheet, (Sport England 2013)

The lifelong legacy of girls' PE 'hatred'

Research links low grades in the subject to poor health in later life.

By David Harrison

It is a familiar scene at many schools: a group of adolescent boys compete to show their prowess on the sports field, while their female peers, perhaps more self-conscious about their bodies, look for any excuse not to take part.

But the reluctance of girls to participate in physical education (PE) could have a damaging effect on their health in later life, a new study has suggested.

A medical researcher in Sweden found that girls who scored low grades in PE experienced more health problems when they were older than girls who achieved high grades.

> **'A lot is being done to widen the curriculum – for example, by introducing dance as a form of PE – and also to ensure that girls wear PE kit that they are comfortable with or that is appropriate to their culture'**

Simon Timpka, from Lund University, also found that girls with poor PE grades faced an increased risk of muscular and skeletal disorders when they were adults. The researcher said he had not found a similar link between boys' grades and health.

Dr Timpka looked at the records of nearly 2,000 people for 30 years, beginning when they were at elementary school. He used detailed population and health data, including statistics on sick leave taken, in-patient care and visits to a doctor, to measure physical impairment. He said, however, that although his study found a link between low PE grades and health problems among women, it did not 'examine or determine' cause and effect.

This suggested that there could be other, undiscovered factors connecting the two, he said. Other influences, such as smoking, obesity or insufficient physical activity 'could potentially explain the observations', he added.

'Girls with a low PE performance may be an important group to target with public health interventions of some sort,' Dr Timpka concludes in his report.

Sue Wilkinson, strategic lead at the Association for Physical Education in the UK, said there was a problem with girls being reluctant 'to engage with physical education' in many schools. 'There is a drop-off at 14 and we have got to work to get them involved,' she said. 'It can be a problem for boys, too, but it seems to be more common among girls, where there are often issues of body image, weight and self-esteem.

'A lot is being done to widen the curriculum – for example, by introducing dance as a form of PE – and also to ensure that girls wear PE kit that they are comfortable with or that is appropriate to their culture.'

But efforts needed to be boosted, Ms Wilkinson said. 'The evidence suggests that, as well as the health benefits, physical education can also improve academic performance.'

Dr Rachel Sandford, lecturer in young people and sport at Loughborough University in England, said that many girls were turned off sport because they thought it would make them look muscular and they associated 'big' with 'fat'.

'That means they will not get the health benefits of being physically active when they are young and, as this new study shows, could suffer health consequences when they get older,' she said. 'Young girls are self-conscious about their body image and it is more of a problem today because they are bombarded with images of the "ideal", which is portrayed as slender. Peer pressure is also a huge factor.'

By contrast, the boys' ideal was more often portrayed as 'strong and muscular', which was more likely to encourage physical activity, she added.

Gary Stidder, principal PE lecturer at the University of Brighton, said that a significant number of teenage girls in particular 'hated' traditional forms of the subject.

He was concerned that the revised national curriculum due to be introduced in England from September 2014, with its emphasis on competitive sport, would 'give the green light to dinosaur games teachers with one ball and a bag of bibs'.

Dr Stidder called for teachers to be more creative and engage girls by offering activities such as yoga, pilates and cheerleading, providing clean changing rooms and allowing girls to choose their own kit.

6 December 2013

Hijab ban threatens basketball phenom

A basketball phenomenon, Bilqis Abdul-Qaadir has always dreamed of a flourishing future as a professional basketball player who has reserved the title of the best player in the state during her high school years.

'As of right now I'm really in a holding pattern because of FIBA,' Abdul-Qaadir told Masslive.com on Thursday, 12 June.

'I think in many ways the key word in FIBA is international. I think that's what upsets me most.'

The youngest of seven children in a devout Muslim family, she was always taught to practise her faith and be proud of whom she was.

And basketball came naturally to her, as she shot hoops as a toddler and kept working at her skills as she grew older, emulating her older brothers.

She was encouraged to put time into her studies as well and remained a top student throughout high school.

During high school, the talented Muslim player made history becoming the top scorer in Massachusetts high school history, breaking the mark of 2,710 points achieved by Women's National Basketball Association star Rebecca Lobo 17 years ago.

Later on, she joined Division I basketball team at the University of Memphis, becoming the first female athlete to play Division I sports – the highest level of sports at the US college level – in full hijab.

Those dreams no longer exist due to the rules of the International Basketball Federation (FIBA).

According to FIBA rules, Islamic headscarf or hijab is banned in matches. The ban was justified by FIBA as a way to remain religiously neutral.

Yet, for Bilqis, these rules mean no chance of playing basketball overseas.

'International means everyone, and FIBA isn't inclusive because of its ban on wearing my hijab,' Abdul-Qaadir said.

'People have this impression of Muslims like they're afraid of us. What some people in the Muslim religion are doing has nothing to do with the rest of us. We're not all the same, just like any religion isn't the same. FIBA says it wants to remain religiously neutral but this is discriminatory.'

Unfair rules

Feeling the injustice of FIBA rules, Abdul-Qaadir expressed insistence to fight for allowing hijab in international games.

'There was an all Muslim women's team that made it to a championship game that FIBA was sponsoring and they wouldn't let them play.

Why engage with faith communities?	Policy and legislation drivers
Faith communities are key agents of change	Specialised units operating within DCLG
Faith communities help to promote personal responsibility and shared values, good citizenship and community cohesion	Tailoring public policy and services to recognise and respect religious differences
Faith communities 'can reach the parts other groups and structures cannot reach'	Encouraging faith communities to contribute to and deliver local services
Volunteering in faith communities is well established and values-driven	Equal opportunities: preventing discrimination on the ground of religion or belief
Key values are a commitment to social justice and helping people in need	Countering extremism, e.g. anti-Semitism and Islamophobia

Source: Section 2 – Understanding faith communities and barriers to sport, Engaging Faith Communities in Sports, Sporting Equals, 2014.

'It just doesn't make any sense to me. It's going to take time for them to change the rules and I'm not going to wait around until they do. I have no plans to change the way I am so I can play basketball. I've come so far and my religion has taken me this far. I'm not going to change.'

The 5-foot-4 Abdul-Qaadir has a master's degree in coaching and seems to have a strong connection to her home town.

'I'd like to find a job somewhere, maybe coach on the high school level,' Abdul-Qaadir said.

'I think I'd like to do that. Even in the next couple of years. I know a place like Commonwealth Academy in Springfield doesn't have a team. They have girls there that might want to play basketball. I think I could go to a place like that and make a difference. We'll see how things go. Right now I'm just trying to weigh my options.'

Though her future career in basketball remained unclear, Bilqis Abdul-Qaadir's name has been recorded as a phenomenon in America's female basketball players.

'I learned a lot along the way,' Abdul-Qaadir said.

'In college you meet a lot of people that aren't like you. I've had a lot of stepping stones, and I really think that everything happens for a reason.'

US Muslims support

The case of young Bilqis has won support for the leading American Muslim advocacy group, Council on American-Islamic Relations (CAIR), which called for allowing hijab in basketball matches.

'Bilqis Abdul-Qaadir, an American Muslim woman who wears an Islamic head scarf (hijab), is unable to pursue a professional career as a basketball player at the international level due to Article 4.4.2 of the FIBA Official Basketball Rules banning "headgear". We believe this rule violates Ms Abdul-Qaadir's religious rights and contravenes international human rights norms,' CAIR wrote in a letter to FIBA President Yvan Mainini.

'No athlete should be forced to choose between faith and sport. Muslim women who seek to participate in sporting activities should not face artificial and arbitrary barriers to that participation.'

The leading Muslim group has also called for negotiations to reach a mutual agreement on athletes' attire.

'The issue of religious attire for athletes can be addressed successfully in a mutually-agreeable manner that maintains the legitimate rights and needs of all parties,' the letter added.

'FIFA's International Football Association Board recently acknowledged the religious rights of athletes by changing its rules to allow hijabs and Sikh turbans.

'As America's largest Muslim civil rights organisation, we formally request that FIBA's Technical Commission meet as soon as possible to discuss changing this discriminatory rule to allow Ms Abdul-Qaadir, and athletes of all faiths, to compete while maintaining religious principles.'

Islam sees hijab as an obligatory code of dress, not a religious symbol displaying one's affiliations.

13 June 2014

⇨ The above information is reprinted with kind permission from OnIslam.net. Please visit www.onislam.net for further information.

Barriers to participation in sport for faith communities

Barriers	Breaking down barriers
Fear of discrimination	Broaden awareness of different faith communities
Attitudes and expectations	Be flexible, avoid stereotypes
Gatekeepers	Develop inclusive partnerships
A perceived lack of sporting ability	Use of appropriate role models to change opinion
Lack of confidence	Build up self-esteem through 'quick wins'
Lack of awareness of opportunities/facilities	Reconsider marketing strategy
Lack of resources	Identify available resources and secure support
Low levels of networking mean that many faith communities are used to supporting their own members, but are less likely to support the wider community	Invest in multi-faith/interfaith events, consult on more effective promotional networks, identify 'sports champions' to take on ambassador role
Patterns of employment – long hours, low pay	Consider when and where consultation should take place so as not to disadvantage anyone because of work
Health – life-limiting illnesses are linked with low incomes and disadvantaged communities	Raise awareness of sport as a means of preventing poor health

Source: Section 2 – Understanding faith communities and barriers to sport, Engaging Faith Communities in Sports, Sporting Equals, 2014.

⇨ Both tables are reprinted with kind permission from Sporting Equals. Please visit www.sportingequals.org.uk for further information. © Sporting Equals 2014

THE CONVERSATION

We don't listen to children when it comes to abuse in sport

An article from The Conversation.

By Jameel Hadi, Lecturer in Social Work at the University of Salford

Sky Sports presenter Charlie Webster has said she revealed details about sexual abuse by her coach when she was young in order to 'break the taboo about abuse as a whole'.

There are certainly issues within sport where too often, poor practice and abuse is tolerated. Who can forget the unravelling of the systematic abuse and cover up of football coach Jerry Sandusky at Penn State and his subsequent jailing for 30 years in 2012?

'The study reported widespread emotionally harmful treatment (75%) and unacceptable levels of sexual harassment (29%)'

A series of high-profile cases, including a British Olympic swimming coach convicted for two rapes, and reports did lead to a change in official procedures and the creation of the NSPCC Child Protection in Sport Unit in 2001. This has driven the adoption of safeguarding standards within sport. But there is no evidence that this process has led to an increased awareness by children about their rights, the behaviour they should expect from adults and who they should turn to if they experience abuse.

A recent study, published by researchers from Edinburgh University and the NSPCC, found that although 'participating in organised sport is a positive experience for most children and young people ... a negative sporting culture exists, is accepted "as the norm" and is perpetuated by peers, coaches and other adults.' The study reported widespread emotionally harmful treatment (75%) and unacceptable levels of sexual harassment (29%).

There are still plenty of anecdotal accounts of children experiencing bullying, adult pressure and exclusion, which has resulted in the Football Association's Respect campaign and grassroots campaigns such as Give us Back our Game.

The implementation of the Children Act 2004 gave emphasis to safeguarding within sport, particularly as this made it clear that promoting the welfare of children was not simply a professional task but the responsibility of all adults, many of whom in sport act in a voluntary capacity. A network of welfare officers now exist on a national, regional and club level in order to promote best practice and to provide a mechanism to deal with complaints or concerns.

For many children sport is a chance to be with friends and experience freedom away from the confines of school or home. This has associated benefits as children who take part in organised activities are more likely to experience a sense of well-being and achieve success. And participating in sports promotes resilience and self-sufficiency. But the way they experience sport is shaped by adults who determine the content, rules and expectations.

'There are still plenty of anecdotal accounts of children experiencing bullying, adult pressure and exclusion...'

Celia Brackenridge, the foremost authority on child protection in sport, said, 'Social control is adeptly applied in youth sport where adults choose, organise, deliver and evaluate activities without inviting comments or contributions from those who consume them – children.'

Being on the winning team

The culture of denial and silence is rooted in the reality that children's sport replicates the professional game where winning is the prime motivation. This means that children compete for spaces in teams and at the elite end are under pressure to conform in order not to undermine their prospects of future success. In this context, to speak out is to risk being left out or incur the displeasure of the coach. A recent *Guardian* article brought into sharp focus the contrast between the glitter of the Premier League when compared to what it termed 'the abuse, death threats, and withering numbers in grassroots football'.

And inevitably, a culture of denial or silence means that bullying, shouting and criticism, exclusion and hostility to opponents can go unchallenged. In Canada when a series of sexual abuse cases came to light in ice hockey, it was found that parent after parent was suspicious of the coach's behaviour and attitude but buried their concerns for fear of scuppering their children's chance at success. On a more routine level, there is a resigned acceptance that poor behaviour and unfair practice is just part of the deal.

Policy vacuum

There is a policy vacuum at national and local level. In 2010 the FA conducted a consultation that suggested that many young people had little or no knowledge of the FA's safeguarding procedures or where they could get more information, advice and support.

Rectifying this will involve creating a culture where young people feel able to set their own priorities. The FA's consultation on youth football included a series of road shows entitled Your Kids, Your Say. But where are the children's voices in this?

Some good things have been happening. A project developed by PTS undertook work on behalf of organisations including the FA, British Judo and Sports Leaders UK to capture the voices of children and resulted in training materials and a film that focused on young people's priorities, such as more say in decisions usually the preserve of adults, such as choosing the captain of a team. The film featured a coach patting all his players on the back after a penalty shootout but ignoring the child who missed the penalty that lost the game. One leading coach said the film should 'have adults squirming on their backsides'.

> **'One ten-year-old said: "The quality of relationships and experience is more important than the outcome."'**

PTS also developed a model of youth leadership, and a children's consultation that identified what was important to children about being in sport and how this related to policies to keep them safe. Children who participated in an FA conference said they wanted an environment of fun, friendship, inclusion and safety that takes precedence over a competitive adult agenda.

One ten-year-old said: 'The quality of relationships and experience is more important than the outcome.' Listening to and involving children is fundamental to ensuring that children speak out. If children are involved in decisions, they are more likely to trust adults and voice concerns.

21 February 2014

⇨ The above information is reprinted with kind permission from The Conversation. Please visit www.theconversation.com for further information.

Sideline Bad Behaviour campaign launched

Children and young people say they are often subjected to intimidating and abusive behaviour from adults as they take part in sport, leading children's charity CHILDREN 1ST reveals today (Monday 20 February).

As they launch the Sideline Bad Behaviour campaign – highlighting the impact of poor behaviour on young players – the charity also revealed that nearly half of all young people who experienced or witnessed aggressive behaviour by spectators at sports games said the abuse continued afterwards (for example on the way to the changing rooms or in the car park).

CHILDREN 1ST conducted a survey of children and young people across Scotland involved in a wide range of sports. The survey, which focused on the behaviour of spectators at sports matches, revealed that swearing and name-calling happened frequently and, in a number of instances, the verbal abuse was threatening. It also revealed that some children under 12 reported being pushed, hit, kicked and punched with the problem of physical violence appearing to get worse for players in their late teens. Almost 20% said poor behaviour from adults affected their performance badly or made them feel like quitting.

In response the charity's national services, Safeguarding in Sport and ParentLine Scotland, are now offering:

⇨ advice for parents and adults worried about their own or other's behaviour

⇨ expert help, resources and child protection training for organisations providing activities for children

⇨ examples of good practice to help tackle poor behaviour

⇨ a special campaign helpline.

One eight-year-old said his game was stopped after an adult confronted the official and the two almost came to blows. He explained: 'It felt scary. We were just standing there. Then they told us to go home. At training next time all they said was "don't worry you won't play that team again until you're older". That didn't really sort anything.'

Young people clearly said that where incidents had occurred they were often ignored or glossed over instead of being acknowledged and dealt with.

One child was told that they were 'a disgrace to the family' following a game in which their team lost. And during another game two parents started fighting while their young school-aged children looked on. In the older age-group (16+), young players reported being physically assaulted by adults.

Alison Todd, Children and Family Services Director at CHILDREN 1ST said: 'Young people used words like "intimidating, angry and scary" to describe the way they were spoken to by adults. There is no other situation where it would be acceptable to treat children like this but in sport it is often excused as "part of the game".

'Through this campaign we're saying that's unacceptable. But we're also offering solutions with advice for parents, resources and training for sports organisations and examples of good practice for people to take on board.'

Advice is just what parents asked for. In a related survey for parents a quarter said they wouldn't know how to challenge poor conduct and nearly 40% said more needed to be done. The ParentLine Scotland service, in conjunction with Safeguarding in Sport, has now produced information and advice – including guidance on how to challenge bad behaviour.

CHILDREN 1ST is also setting up a special campaign helpline through ParentLine Scotland to handle calls from anyone concerned about poor behaviour on the sidelines of children's sporting activities and events. The free and confidential helpline can provide information, advice and support to anyone worried about their own behaviour or the behaviour of others to help them deal with it and create more positive experiences for children and young people participating in sport. The number is 0141 418 5674.

Safeguarding in Sport, who work with a number of key sports organisations, aim to repeat the surveys in 18–24 months, time to see if there has been a shift in attitudes to how children are treated in sport.

Key findings from research with children and young people:

⇨ 43% have had direct experience of bad behaviour by spectators.

⇨ 47% said they had witnessed bad behaviour affecting other players.

⇨ Swearing and name calling was the most common form of bad behaviour.

⇨ All the children who took part in interviews and/or focus groups said they felt threatened by verbal abuse they witnessed or experienced.

⇨ Children who took part in the survey identified at least 21 separate instances when they had been subject to physical abuse, including pushing, kicking, hitting and spitting.

⇨ A small but significant number of children under 12 said they had been kicked, hit, punched or pushed (seven incidents reported).

⇨ 13% of participants said they had felt scared and intimidated

⇨ One in five (19%) said the bad behaviour adversely affected their performance or made them want to quit.

⇨ Nearly half of those young people who experienced or witnessed bad behaviour said it continued after the activity finished (e.g. on the way to the changing rooms).

⇨ Our analysis of responses by age range found that the number of incidents involving bad behaviour, and the seriousness of the behaviour, escalates as the children become older.

Key findings from research with parents and carers:

⇨ Half of all respondents confirmed that their child had mentioned poor behaviour by spectators.

⇨ 43% of parents said they had witnessed bad behaviour.

⇨ The most commonly reported bad behaviour was swearing at children, calling them names and making fun of them.

⇨ Just over two thirds (68%) of parents reported that someone challenged the bad behaviour. But one in four parents (25%) said they would not know what to do to tackle bad behaviour

⇨ 38% of parents agreed that more needs to be done to address this problem.

Quotes from children and young people:

'I've been threatened with: "I'm going to stab you after the game". None of the adults did anything about it.'

'You get comments when you walk past parents. It's a horrible part of the game but it's just accepted.'

'Two mums had a go at each other. It started as a laugh but it kicked off. It was really nasty, horrible, one kid standing nearby started crying.'

'I'm Scottish but my dad is from Pakistan and I get quite a lot of racist comments going on. But nobody ever seems to do anything about it – I think they're scared to tackle it. I can't stand it when adults laugh when another adult makes a racist remark.'

'[As I've got older] ... the verbal stuff gets worse too, more serious, threatening comments, like: "I'll get you later, you're marked, you'd better watch your back." And this is from the adults!'

'I don't want to be bad-mouthed by the opposition when you do something good.'

'If parents can't say positive stuff then they shouldn't come to the games.'

'My dad's the best role model I could ask for. He was always on the touchline giving me great support and always encouraging me on – really good, really positive. He's just an inspiration for me.'

Quotes from parents:

'I heard one parent tell their child they were a disgrace to the family.'

'All of the abusive ones are sadly part of the game. Coaches and parents alike are guilty of participating and encouraging this behaviour.'

'I've seen two parents fight as their primary school-aged children looked on.'

Sideline Bad Behaviour helpline number: 0141 418 5674 (Monday–Friday, 9am–5pm)

About Safeguarding in Sport

CHILDREN 1ST has operated a national service promoting child protection in sport since 2001, with the support and backing of sportscotland. Safeguarding in Sport provides advice, information and guidance to Scottish sports governing bodies, local authorities, coaches and club officials. The service has a national helpline and manages a series of network meetings involving professional staff and volunteers responsible for developing sport in communities throughout Scotland. It also delivers child protection training (at basic and advanced levels) through a network of accredited tutors. The website www.safeguardinginsport.org.uk has become an authoritative reference point for everyone involved in sport seeking guidance and support on safeguarding children in sport.

20 February 2012

⇨ The above information is reprinted with kind permission from CHILDREN 1ST, the charity which runs Safeguarding in Sport. Please visit www.children1st.org.uk for further information.

Plight of steroid users highlighted

More must be done to help the rising tide of people who are injecting themselves with steroids, health experts have warned.

Reports suggest the number of people, including teenagers, who use steroids and other performance or image-enhancing drugs is 'rapidly increasing', the National Institute for Health and Care Excellence (NICE) said.

Outreach programmes should be set up in gyms to try to reach this group of drug users, NICE said.

In new guidance, the health authority said that needle and syringe programmes – which were set up in the 1980s and 1990s to stem the spread of HIV – should also make sure that these drug users have the sterile equipment they need to prevent the spread of blood-borne viruses.

Meanwhile, local health bodies need to increase the proportion of these drug users who are tested for HIV, hepatitis B and C and other viruses.

People who use these drugs do not see themselves as having a drug problem, a NICE spokesman said.

In fact, they see themselves as 'fit and healthy' despite the fact that people who inject themselves with any type of drug are at a heightened risk of HIV and hepatitis.

NICE warned that anabolic steroid use is 'relatively widespread' with an estimated 59,000 people aged 16 to 59 using the drug in England and Wales in the last year.

But NICE said these estimates are 'conservative' and said that needle and syringe programmes have reported 'rapidly increasing' numbers of steroid users attending their services.

David Rourke, harm reduction lead for Arundel Street Project – a needle and syringe programme in Sheffield, said: 'We run a weekly clinic for steroid users but we have people coming through the door on a daily basis, with at least seven new clients a week. We know there are many more people out there who are not using needle and syringe programmes because this group of users do not see themselves as drug users. Traditionally, they are more sexually active than users of heroin or crack, so there is more potential for the spread of infections through sex.

'This guideline gives front-line workers clear recommendations on how to support image and performance-enhancing drug users. Up to now this has been a grey area; services around the country have been patchy to say the least.

'In Sheffield we are lucky to have a special programme for those who use steroids to access information and support but I know of some areas where there is nothing.

'People who inject steroids are potentially using them without the correct education or the correct equipment and this can lead to more and more people injecting unsafely, which can put not just their own life, but the lives of those around them, at risk.

'Those who use steroids should be able to get the same support as anyone else who injects drugs. This guideline will make sure that services across the country are at the high standard they should be.'

Professor Mike Kelly, director of NICE's Centre for Public Health, added: 'Needle and syringe programmes have been a huge success story in the UK, they are credited with helping stem the AIDS epidemic in the '80s and '90s. However, we are now seeing a completely different group of people injecting drugs.

'They do not see themselves as "drug addicts"; quite the contrary, they consider themselves to be fit and healthy people who take pride in their appearance.

'Since we last published our guideline on needle and syringe programmes in 2009, we've seen an increase in the use of image and performance-enhancing drugs such as anabolic steroids. We've also heard anecdotal evidence that more teenagers are injecting these image and performance-enhancing drugs too. We're updating our guideline to make sure all of these groups of people are considered in the planning and delivery of needle and syringe programmes.'

Dr Fortune Ncube, head of the blood-borne virus section, at Public Health England's National Centre for Infectious Disease Surveillance and Control, added: 'Anyone who injects drugs is at risk of HIV and other blood-borne viruses, regardless of the substance they inject.

'Our recent research suggests that levels of HIV and hepatitis infection among men using image and performance-enhancing drugs have increased since the 1990s.

'We must maintain and strengthen public health interventions focused on reducing injection-related risk behaviours to prevent HIV and hepatitis infections in this group. This includes ensuring easy access for those who inject image and performance-enhancing drugs to voluntary confidential testing services for HIV and hepatitis and vaccination against hepatitis B, as well as to appropriate sterile injecting equipment through needle and syringe programmes.'

Mark Moody, director of operations at health and social care charity CRI (Crime Reduction Initiatives), said: 'Needle exchanges help to prevent the spread of blood-borne viruses like HIV and hepatitis C by giving people who inject drugs clean equipment and advice. In the long term, it also provides an opportunity for us to engage with people with problematic substance misuse to create new pathways to recovery.

'Every contact at a needle exchange is a chance for us to support recovery and our staff work hard to address specific issues and refer people to further support. This new NICE guideline will ensure that our staff are using the most up-to-date evidence available in their work. We particularly welcome the recommendations to involve people who use services and local communities in developing needle exchange programmes, as well as tailoring services to meet local need.'

9 April 2014

⇨ The above information is reprinted with kind permission from the *Telegraph & Argus* and the Press Association. Please visit www.thetelegraphandargus.co.uk for further information.

Dangers of doping

What's the big deal?

Most medications on the Prohibited List can be bought at a pharmacy – so they must be safe to use, right?

NO! Medications are for people with specific health issues – not healthy athletes. They were not approved to be used by healthy people, in higher doses and in combination with other substances.

What about dietary or nutritional supplements?

'All-natural. Pure fast results.' BEWARE!

Supplement companies are not highly regulated – meaning you never know what you are taking. There could be a banned substance in your 'all-natural' supplement.

What's at risk?

All medications have side effects – but taking them when your body doesn't need them can cause serious damage to your body and destroy your athletic career.

What else should you know?

Methods

There are also methods of administering substances or manipulating your physiology that are banned. These methods can also have negative effects on your body. For example, blood doping, including having blood transfusions to change the way your blood carries oxygen to the rest of your body, may result in:

⇨ An increased risk of heart failure, stroke, kidney damage and high blood pressure

⇨ Problems with your blood – like infections, poisoning, overloading of your white cells and reduction of platelet count

⇨ Problems with your circulatory system.

HIV/AIDS

As with any injectable drug, using a syringe to dope puts you at a higher risk for contracting infectious diseases such as HIV/AIDS and hepatitis.

What happens to an athlete who uses?

Steroids

Steroids may make your muscles big and strong, BUT... you may become dependent on them and they may:

⇨ Give you acne

⇨ Make you bald

⇨ Increase your risk of liver and cardiovascular disease

⇨ Give you mood swings

⇨ Make you more aggressive

⇨ Make you suicidal.

Guys, you may also look forward to:

⇨ Shrinking testicles

⇨ Breast growth

⇨ Reduced sex drive and even impotence

⇨ Decrease in sperm production.

Ladies, you may look forward to:

⇨ Deeper voice

⇨ Excessive facial and body hair

⇨ Abnormal menstrual cycles

⇨ An enlarged clitoris.

EPO

EPO (erythropoietin) may help with the way your body uses oxygen, BUT... why risk it when it may lead to death?

Using EPO may make your blood more like honey – thick and sticky – than water. Trying to pump this thick blood through your veins may:

⇨ Make you feel weak – not good when you are trying to train hard!

⇨ Give you high blood pressure

⇨ Make your heart work so hard that you have a heart attack of stroke (even at your age).

Stimulants

Stimulants are used to heighten the competitive edge, BUT... how edgy would you feel if you:

⇨ Can't sleep (insomnia)

⇨ Have involuntary shaking or trembling

⇨ Have problems with your coordination and balance

- Are anxious and aggressive
- Develop an increased and irregular heart rate
- Have a heart attack (imagine dying of a heart attack at your age!) or stroke.

These are the effects that using stimulants may have on your body.

HGH

HGH (human growth hormone) may make muscles and bones stronger and recover faster, BUT... it is not only your muscles that get bigger.

Using HGH may lead to:

- Acromegaly – protruding forehead, brow, skull and jaw – which can't be reversed
- An enlarged heart that can result in high blood pressure and even heart failure
- Damage to your liver, thyroid and vision
- Crippling arthritis.

Masking agents

Some athletes try to cheat the system by using diuretics and other substances to cover-up the signs of using banned substances.

The side effects can definitely affect your ability to compete and train. You may:

- Become dizzy or even faint
- Become dehydrated
- Get muscle cramps
- Have a drop in blood pressure
- Lose coordination and balance
- Become confused and moody
- Develop cardiac disorders.

Marijuana

Marijuana, cannabis, pot – whatever you call it, IT IS BANNED. Whether you are a port-head or a casual user, marijuana may have a negative effect on your athletic performance and your health.

Using may:

- Reduce your memory, attention and motivations – even result in learning disabilities
- Weaken your immune system
- Affect your lungs (chronic bronchitis and other respiratory diseases, even throat cancer)
- Lead to psychological and physical dependence.

Narcotics

Narcotics, like heroin and morphine, may help you forget about the pain, BUT... how competitive do you think you'd be with a:

- Weakened immune system
- Decreased heart rate and suppressed respiratory system (you can't compete if you are dead)
- Loss in balance, coordination and concentration
- Gastrointestinal problem like vomiting and constipation
- Narcotics are also highly addictive – your body and mind quickly become dependent on them.
- Source: World Anti-Doping Agency's (WADA) 'Dangers of Doping Leaflet'. Please note that the original version can be found on WADA's website at the following link: http://www.wada-ama.org/Documents/Education_Awareness/Tools?Dangers_of_Doping_Leaflet/WADA_Dangers_of_Doping_EN.pdf

Match-fixing creates a dark cloud over English football

A dark cloud has descended over the beautiful game in recent weeks as several match-fixing scandals spread across the news.

By Ellen Farrell

As the days go by, more and more scandals are being brought to the public's attention with former AC Milan player, Gattuso, the most recent high-profile footballer to have allegedly been involved in match-fixing in Serie A.

This follows on from Sam Sodje, an ex-Portsmouth player, telling an undercover reporter he could arrange yellow and red cards in exchange for money and Blackburn's DJ Campbell being arrested along with six other people in connection with allegations of match and spot-fixing.

This is not the first time that a match-fixing scandal has plagued the world of football. Just in February of this year, Europol identified 380 matches in Europe which were claimed to have been fixed and a further 300 more around the world. Their investigation recognised 425 suspects and 50 people were arrested. There was even the allegation by a Turkish official that the Champions League, Europe's most prestigious club competition, was fixed by using vibrating balls for the draw.

Match-fixing is a serious criminal problem which is a threat to the integrity and reputation of sport and is a growing concern within football. The commercialisation and globalisation of football has arguably transformed it into a marketable commodity, making it attractive for big investors who perceive it as an enterprise where money can be generated and footballing empires created. However, the presence of capitalism and commercialism in football has fuelled the proliferation of money-making motives and match-fixing provides an opportunity for a lot of money to be made.

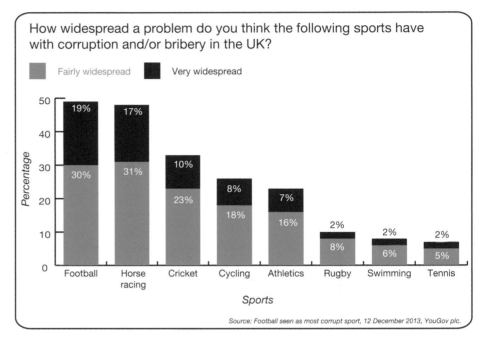

How widespread a problem do you think the following sports have with corruption and/or bribery in the UK?

Source: Football seen as most corrupt sport, 12 December 2013, YouGov plc.

Out of the 380 suspicious European matches identified in the Europol investigation, more than £8 million was generated in betting profits and more than £2 million was paid in bribes. Footballers themselves can make money from it, especially through spot-fixing where they manipulate a certain aspect of the game. Players become greedy and therefore may happily accept money for arranging to help fix matches despite their large wage packets. Former Southampton player Matt Le Tissier admitted taking part in a bet which could have netted him £10,000 for kicking the ball out of play at a certain time in a premier league match against Wimbledon in 1995.

Match-fixing challenges and undermines the fundamental values which sport prides itself upon such as fair play, respect and honesty. Moreover, it sabotages the exciting and uncertain element of surprise that sport creates and so football is in danger of becoming a corrupt institution.

A leading FIFA official, Jerome Valcke, labelled match fixing a disease which could kill the sport if nothing is done to eradicate it. FIFA has recognised the threat that match fixing poses to the integrity of football and has recently launched a £17.5 million ten-year partnership with Interpol in a bid to combat it.

It is vital that this dark cloud is lifted but, as recent events demonstrate, more needs to be done to fight the 'disease' which is contaminating football before it kills the beautiful game.

24 December 2013

⇨ The above information is reprinted with kind permission from The Offside Rule. Please visit www.offsiderulepodcast.com for further information.

Video games: the sport of the future?

They're idolised by millions, perform amazing mental and physical feats, and can earn a fortune. But will the professional gamer stars of 'eSports' ever reach the premier league? Chris Bell reports.

At a packed arena in Seoul, the atmosphere is electric. More than 30,000 fans are glued to the stage's vast video screen. On a speedboat racing down the city's Han river, their champion is approaching. Known as 'BoxeR', he is 27 years old, fantastically wealthy and a national hero.

By the time he emerges onstage – popping out of the floor in an explosion of lasers and pyrotechnics – the screaming has reached ear-bleeding levels. But BoxeR, dressed in military-style white tunic, spiked hair framed by silver headphones, stares at the crowd impassively. He has work to do.

Finally, he sits down. An expectant hush descends across the arena – not to mention among the million viewers watching online, or via dedicated cable channels. BoxeR pulls out a keyboard, waiting for the signal. A klaxon sounds. He begins to type.

And click. And move. And mine. And build. The screen flashes with bewildering action. His fingers dancing across the keyboard in knuckle-dislocating combinations, BoxeR starts to attack. The audience roar. He attacks again, and again. And 'pow!' – within 15 minutes, he has entirely obliterated the Zerg, a despicable race of aliens. The crowd go bananas; BoxeR raises his arm, victorious.

Which is a little galling. Especially if you were a child of the eighties and nineties, and told by your parents that you'd never amount to anything if you sat around playing Super Mario 2 all day. Or maybe, like many gamers, you write off the odd bout of Call of Duty as a time-wasting pleasure. Either way: more fool you.

Because you may not have heard of BoxeR, also known as Lim Yo-Hwan. Or Hong Jin-Ho, whose fingers are insured for £38,000. Or 19-year-old Lee 'MarineKing' Jung Hoon, or Jang 'MC' Min Chul, 21. But they, and dozens like them, typify the rise

of a curious new sportsman: the professional video game player. People capable of earning millions of pounds a year simply for their ability to twiddle a joypad, or wrangle a mouse.

Of course, competitive gaming is nothing new. Back in 1982, the American television show *Starcade* featured competitions among arcade game players. Channel 4's *Gamesmaster* held regular gaming competitions under the fierce monocular gaze of a distorted Patrick Moore.

It was during the nineties, however, that multiplayer competitions really took off. It began with secretive LAN (Local Area Network) parties where players would connect their computers directly and play the first-person shooter game Unreal Tournament. Later, as the Internet developed past the squeak and buzz of dial-up, these parties could stretch across continents. But it's only been in the last ten years that competitive gaming has seen star players and million-pound sponsorships.

That South Korea is the epicentre may come as no surprise. Ever since the Government rolled out high-speed fibre optic broadband in the late nineties, an estimated four million Koreans (from a population of just 50 million) are playing online games at any given moment. And StarCraft – a PC strategy game that looks, to the untrained eye, like a bewildering combination of Risk, speed chess and a riot – quickly grew to be the national sport.

Today, three dedicated cable television channels broadcast matches 24 hours a day. Samsung and Coca-Cola clamour for sponsorship deals, pushing prize funds to over £2.6 million. And players like BoxeR have cleaned up. His career prize money has passed £320,000. He has a fan club with 490,000 registered members. A DVD of his winning

tactics in 2003 outsold the film *Matrix: Revolutions*.

In a country where the average annual salary is just £10,000, it's no wonder he's a sporting icon. All of which has led many observers to ponder the question: when will it happen over here? When will 'eSports' mature from being some esoteric, nerdish peculiarity of the technophile East, and reach the mainstream media of the West?

The answer is: it already has. Thanks to live streaming – allowing fans to watch tournaments over the Internet – eSports has quietly become a multimillion-dollar industry in Europe and the United States, featuring major global events attended by thousands and watched by millions. It's something that TL Taylor, an associate professor at MIT, has scrutinised closely. As author of *Raising the Stakes: E-Sports and the Professionalisation of Computer Gaming*, she asserts that gaming has moved beyond a 'niche' activity. 'Competitive gaming is claiming a space similar to that of traditional sport,' she says. 'The rise of live streaming has turned on its head the idea that major networks need to be the ultimate venue for this stuff.'

So instead of the usual evidence of mainstream recognition – a slot on Saturday prime-time television, say, hosted by Holly Willoughby – competitive gaming has carved out a far more lucrative and loyal fan base online. Websites like Twitch. tv or GameSpot (notably owned by American television network CBS) regularly attract audiences of over 200,000. That's bigger than most Sky channels.

The status of gaming is growing every year. The first-person shooter franchises – such as Call of Duty or Halo – are wildly popular. This year's Call of Duty: Black Ops championship in April was held in Los Angeles, with teams competing for $1 million. And, as in Korea, the best players rake in the cash. Current Call of Duty champion Matthew 'NaDeSHoT' Haag is sponsored by Red Bull and is worth $400,000, while former champion Johnathan 'Fatal1ty' Wendel retired aged 32, after earning $500,000 in prize money and launching his own branded motherboards.

And yet the most popular games are, arguably, the least spectator friendly. Known as Mobas, or Massive Online Battle Arenas, they're the modern incarnation of a Dungeons and Dragons-style statistic-based fighting game – complex and baffling. And yet the biggest of them all, League of Legends, has more than 70 million players. That huge inbuilt fan base contributed to making last October's final the most watched eSports event ever – with more than eight million viewers watching in 13 languages. Put it this way: *The Voice* would kill for figures like that.

And the number of eSports tournaments worldwide grows every year: from the Olympic-esque World Cyber Games to the Evo Championship Series, the European Gaming League and so on. One of the biggest American communities is Major League Gaming with eight million members. The CEO of MLG, Sundance DiGiovanni, thinks the West is close to catching up with the mania of South Korea.

'At our Pro Circuit Championship events, we get over 1,000 players competing for hundreds of thousands in prize money,' he says. 'We have thousands turning out for events and millions watching online. As viewership continues to grow, I think we'll see the mainstream media taking notice.' The inevitable consequence is increasing numbers of professional gamers – even here in Britain. Take, for example, Michael O'Dell. Or, as he was known when playing for the British national team, 'Odee'. Having left school aged 16, he started playing first-person shooters like Quake and Battlefield 1942 after injuring his knee playing football.

Now 41, he quit his 'normal job' as a sales and marketing manager in 2006 to become CEO of the largest pro-gaming collective in Europe:

the slightly morbidly named Team Dignitas. 'We wanted a cool Latin phrase,' he admits sheepishly. 'We didn't realise the connection until after we'd registered the company. It was a bit awkward.' And yet despite the overtones of oblivion, Team Dignitas is booming. The roster includes 67 players of 14 nationalities, including American and Korean players. And O'Dell himself spends his time flitting between the team's head office – his converted garage in Surrey – and the Team Dignitas gaming house: a $1 million mansion in Los Angeles, full of players practising League of Legends 24 hours a day.

All of which O'Dell has recruited. 'I'm a bit of an Alex Ferguson figure,' he says grudgingly (he's an Arsenal fan), 'I'm constantly on the lookout for new talent. I'm currently trying to bring a Ukrainian World of Tanks team on board.' For him, the business plan is simple. Money comes in from cash prizes, corporate sponsorship and the ad revenue from online matches. 'Streaming has revolutionised how people watch eSports,' he says. 'Even away from the tournaments, top players can make $60–70,000 a year just screening tutorials to people online.' One pro-gamer, a World of Warcraft expert called Athene, boasts over 600,000 subscribers to his YouTube channel AtheneWins. His 600-plus videos have been viewed over 323 million times. 'It's the equivalent of a webcam at Man United's training ground,' says O'Dell.

Nevertheless, he warns, most of his young players aren't paid a penny; Team Dignitas merely pays for flights and board so they can attend tournaments around the globe. But his premier league players – those excelling at League of Legends, for example – can expect a £40,000 salary. 'They're genuinely famous,' he says. 'After a tournament in Texas earlier this year, the team were signing autographs for an hour and a half. And yes, there are groupies I have to fend off so they can train properly. I'm no different to any other sport manager.'

Which brings us onto the other multimillion dollar question: will competitive gaming ever be recognised as a sport in its own right? This may seem laughable for

an activity based around staring at a monitor. But, TL Taylor argues, pro-gamers require a level of dedication akin to athletics. 'The key components are all there,' she says.

'Measurable and differential skills, advanced tactical and strategic thinking, physical and material components and formal and informal structures of competition to name just a few.' O'Dell claims his players practise for 'eight to ten hours a day, usually more'; South Korean teams are known to train for 17 hours a day, 350 days a year. And that's not just to avoid sunlight or talking to girls.

StarCraft, for example, is played by issuing commands – selecting a particular military unit, then ordering it to attack a specific enemy. However, to beat everyone else requires doing this hundreds of times a minute – which means practising combinations of keystrokes and mouse movements over and over again.

Pro-gamers measure this in APM, or actions per minute. Most casual StarCraft players manage an APM of between 50 and 70. The infamous BoxeR regularly hits 400 APM. That's 6.66 unique sequences of keystrokes and mouse movements per second. 'People may make fun of what we do,' says O'Dell, 'but try getting that right in a split second in front of 30,000 people.' Perhaps it's no wonder, then, that other countries have moved to put joypad mastery on a par with football or athletics. The South Korean Government actively supports the Korean Pro-Gamers Association, while in Denmark, gaming teams can apply for tax breaks and social housing. O'Dell himself, as a member of the Ukie (The UK Interactive Entertainment Association), will next month meet with British MPs to educate them about the gaming scene. Although he suspects official recognition is unlikely. 'Just the way the Sports Council is set up,' he says, 'I can't see it happening yet.'

In the end, though, it will be the quietly burgeoning popularity that drives recognition. Not just at the highest levels of government, but also in the minds of concerned parents everywhere. 'It's not quite a solid career option yet,' admits

O'Dell. 'While the infrastructure is there, it needs time to develop. The gaming world also needs to get more female-friendly. There are lots of good female players, but we need more. Gaming is the ultimate level playing field – there's no reason why girls can't beat guys.

'And when the right guy comes along, who's good-looking and charismatic enough, I'm convinced he'll achieve the status and wealth of someone like David Beckham. Honestly,' he smiles, 'it makes you want to be 18 again.'

26 June 2013

⇨ The above information is reprinted with kind permission from *The Telegraph*. Please visit www.telegraph.co.uk for further information.

Why sporting head injuries must be taken seriously

Sportsmen may think they are indestructible, but it's vital that we pay attention to signs of concussion and head injury, says Dr Phil Hammond.

By Phil Hammond

If a sportsman (or indeed anyone) who's been whacked on the head answers 'I can't remember' to the question 'Were you knocked out?', take them away from further harm (i.e. off the pitch).

It's a simple and obvious decision to prevent the human brain (essentially a life-critical blancmange in a box) from sustaining further damage, and to allow further careful assessment of any harm already done.

Alas, professional sportsmen are not always blessed with great judgement, especially after a head-on collision, and the pressure to play on may be huge if the reserve goalkeeper is a fumble-fingers. That's why we invented doctors. To tell us what to do, based on the best available evidence, to prevent further harm. Of course, this only works if doctors follow the guidelines, managers and players take notice of the doctors and referees have the courage and authority to order a player to be replaced for his own safety if he's refusing to go.

But let's start with the guidelines. If anyone (kid, adult, male, female) shows any signs of concussion (severe blancmange wobble) after any injury, they need to be properly assessed by someone qualified to do so. This could either be at the pitch side if a doctor or paramedic is available or in hospital.

The things to look for are loss of consciousness (however short-lived), stumbling or unsteadiness on the feet, not knowing where they are or what the time or day is, confused or hesitant answers, or looking completely vacant. Some sportsmen have some of these characteristics all the time. It's the subtle or dramatic changes you're looking for.

Head injuries sometimes go with neck injuries, particularly in rugby where the tackler has got his head in the wrong place or a scrum has collapsed. So it's really important to get an expert assessment if you think this has happened before you move a player.

Both FIFA and the International Rugby Board print their own clear guidance on this which all pitchside first-aiders should carry and follow. The IRB, set up a protocol two seasons ago requiring a player who had suffered a head injury to go off the field for a five-minute assessment. This wasn't for concussion to be diagnosed – it can take far longer and require more observation – but to gauge whether it might be a possibility. Any suspicion and the player should not return to the field.

Sadly anyone who's played rugby for any length of time will have known of someone who came off with a head injury, seemed alright during beers after the game and then was later found dead in his bed. I remember this happening to a fellow student at university. The real danger of head collisions is often the slow bleed of torn blood vessels combined with swelling of the brain that isn't immediately obvious.

Anyone who has suffered concussion should not be left alone for up to 48 hours after their injury. This is possible if you have a partner but the single student or young bloke living alone is at high risk. This is when you realise a team sport extends beyond the game. If a friend has been hit in the head, get him off the pitch and get a proper medical assessment.

Don't go out on the beer, go home and stay with him for a night or two. You're looking out for a headache that gets worse, blurred vision, drowsiness and confusion. If it happens, get help urgently. Sportsmen can pretend to be indestructible, but they're not. And however much muscle you have, your brain will always be a blancmange in a box.

15 November 2013

⇨ The above information is reprinted with kind permission from *The Telegraph*. Please visit www.telegraph.co.uk for further information.

The psychological effect of injury

By Gavin Teehan

Injury is part and parcel of a sports person's life. No one goes through their career without suffering some form of injury. How you cope with it can define who you are as a person and whether or not you ever fully recover. Everything from a minor knock to a full-on career-ending injury impacts the individual psychologically and directly affects their future performance. In fact, not only are the individuals affected, but often those around them too. Family, friends, colleagues and team-mates have an important part to play on the often lonely road to recovery. A good support network can be as vital as a good physio!

What I propose to do is to have a look at injury from a number of perspectives, including young and mature players, social and professional players. It's very difficult to have a one-size-fits-all answer to how each injury affects the individual. I myself spent a lifetime playing and injuries of all shapes and sizes were part of the daily grind. I will use some of these injuries, along with others that I have witnessed, as a reference point for some of my opinions.

While I use football for most of my examples (it's what I know and love), many of these situations can be mirrored in other sports.

Scenario 1: Young player beginning to learn the game

The first time a young player gets hurt is a vital part of their development. While it can initially lead them to say that they don't want to play the game any more, a natural reaction perhaps considering this shock to the system, they must experience such things to learn. They need to understand that bumps and bruises are part of the game and generally don't do any long-term damage. A few tears are OK and an arm around the shoulder from mum or dad can often help. However, you can't cocoon the players forever. Not only do they need to understand that physical contact is nothing to fear, they also need to learn how to protect themselves.

Scenario 2: Teenager playing at a high level

A player at this level will have experienced a variety of injuries from cuts and bruises, to twists and sprains. Thankfully, serious injury at this stage of a career is rare but players at this age see any injury that keeps them from playing as catastrophic! It is vital that players understand the correct stages of rehabilitation. Rushing back from an injury too soon can often lead to further problems down the line and ultimately more time on the side-lines. Young players can often feel weak or stupid for being injured at all and can become annoyed with themselves for not being strong enough to cope with the physical side of the game. It is vital that coaches, managers and parents alike stress the fact that injuries are unavoidable and in no way their own fault. Players should be helped back to full fitness by a qualified physio and not simply rely on old wives tales as to the right things to do. The reason I mention this is that years ago a team-mate of mine was told to wrap their ankle in vinegar and brown paper due to a severe pain they had in their ankle. The player did this for a whole week before finally giving in and going to the hospital… Only to discover they had a stress fracture!

Scenario 3: Teenager playing socially

Players at this level often look on an injury as a badge of honour. They love the fact that they will miss a few games and secretly don't mind the break. They often only play the game because their mates do too… or they are forced to do so… so missing game time doesn't upset them too much at all. Psychologically, the injury can actually make them feel good, as it earns them street credibility and the much sought after, sympathy vote! A friend of mine spent a little longer on his crutches than needed, because of the attention he was getting from some female admirers!

Scenario 4: Young adult playing professionally

This is probably the player affected most by an injury. At this point in their life, their sport is everything, the majority of the time, to the detriment of everything else. They view injury as a major speed bump in their life, they go above and beyond the call of duty to get back to full playing fitness. Players at this level live to play and can be affected strongly by the time away from their team-mates and the endless hours of rehab in the gym. An injury for this player tests them to the limits and only the very strong single minded come back stronger than pre-injury.

I myself underwent nine knee operations from the age of 20 to 28. It tested my mental strength greatly and made me a better person for having to deal with such adversity from a young age. With every operation I became wiser as to what to do to recover faster and stronger, but it did make me feel as low as I could ever had imagined at times, thinking that I would never regain the fitness or form that I had displayed prior to the injury.

Scenario 5: Young adult playing socially

An injury for this player can end their involvement in the game. Not because the injury is so severe that they can't recover, more for the fact that they may miss work or can't afford the time off. Many players' careers ended because social responsibility to kids and partners came before fulfilling longstanding football ambitions. I have a string of friends who retired simply because it wasn't worth it any more…

Scenario 6: Mature player playing professionally

An injury to this type of player is often taken in their stride. Many players at this level have accepted that their days are numbered and if clever enough, have already begun plotting the next phase of their life. Players at this level don't seem to get as upset by the layoff and if anything seem to maximise the potential to get time in the gym to build strength and recuperate. Players like this still however harbour the fact that they will return and this sets them apart from the player who has no hope of playing again. I will come to this player in due course...

Scenario 7: Mature player playing socially

Much like the young adult playing socially, this player plays for fun above all else. The game is not life or death and an injury, no matter how small can sway the balance towards retirement in an instant. The game owes the player nothing at this stage and vice versa. Injury is more of a nuisance that interferes with all other aspects of their lives than anything else.

Scenario 8: Career-ending injury

Players who find themselves at this stage of their careers, regardless of age, can find it hard to accept their fate. Having spent most of their time training and playing the game, to suddenly having it removed, can be a culture shock to say the least. When I did finally retire at 28, I felt angry for a long time and turned my back on football for about two years. I felt that other players were still playing who did not appreciate what they had and wished that I could still play. The injury became like an enemy and I hated even talking about it. In time I learned to accept that there were many other avenues to explore to keep me involved and coaching filled a huge hole in my footballing life.

Simple as all of these examples are, I hope that they give you an idea of how injury can affect players. No matter what your age or what your level, injury should not be dealt with alone. Seek the help of medical professionals and the support of friends and family. The road to full recovery can be a lonely one, but ultimately a rewarding one. Treat each injury as your next opponent. Do your homework and work out its strengths and weaknesses. Formulate you own game plan to beat it but never forget the way it made you feel. Draw on these feelings and learn to be a better, mentally stronger player.

23 May 2013

⇨ The above information is reprinted with kind permission from TheSportinMind. Please visit www.thesportinmind.com for further information.

Where next for secondary school sport?

Despite all the talk of Olympic legacy, funding for secondary school sport runs dry this September. Former PE teacher and sports coach Crispin Andrews looks back at two years of sporting cuts and asks what next?

Little over six months after London handed the Olympic torch to Rio, arguments about government funding of school sport rage on.

This September will see the second anniversary of the day that £168 million a year in funding, which enabled every maintained school in the country to be part of a School Sports Partnership (SSP), ran out.

In 2009/10, more than 90 per cent of pupils had two hours of PE a week and 78 per cent took part in competitive sport. Despite this, thousands of school sports co-ordinators, partnership development managers, competition managers and primary link teachers lost their jobs when the cuts hit. Those who remained were required to return to a narrower focus on their own classes and sports teams.

The 2010 public service spending review also removed sports college funding. Local authorities, too, had their budgets cut and leisure and recreation, seen by many local decision-makers as a non-essential service, was one of the areas hardest hit.

The Government also abolished PE and school sports targets. Before that, schools whose children did two or more hours of PE at school had their names published and the school sports movement, headed up by the Youth Sport Trust, was well on its way towards achieving five hours a week.

Elsewhere, guidelines that linked a school's playing field(s) size to its number of pupils on roll have gone. Now headteachers can decide what a 'suitable' outdoor playing space might look like and while many school leaders will maintain their outdoor areas, there are concerns that balancing budgets and generating revenue might be just as big an influence on decisions as providing the best environment for children to play sport.

There have been glimmers of hope. For the last two years, secondary school heads have had some extra funding to release a PE teacher from their own teaching timetable, one day a week, to organise sport. A compromise offered by the Government after the outcry over its SSP cuts.

For the past two years, these teachers have spent their time in their own school or, if the head and their PE department was so inclined, in local primaries. This money was not ring-fenced, though. If the headteacher wanted to use it to refurbish changing rooms or employ an extra music teacher, they could, although this funding is set to run out at the end of this academic year.

In January 2011, the Government also announced that Sport England will help set up 4,000 community sports clubs on secondary school sites, where expert coaches will run sessions to create ties between schools and existing local sports clubs. Already, 2,000 football clubs have pledged to be linked to secondary schools by 2017, 1,300 rugby union clubs, 1,250 cricket clubs and 1,000 rugby league and tennis clubs.

However, in March, the Government's long-awaited school sports announcement disappointed many secondaries – a new £150 million primary school sport initiative with funding from both the Departments of Health and Education. This is ring-fenced money which will be given directly to primary schools over the next two years to be spent on sport. And there's enough of it, the Government says, for an average-sized primary of 250 children, to employ a specialist teacher or coach for two days a week.

Whereas before, funding and expertise filtered down to primaries through the SSPs and secondary schools, now primary schools will go it alone.

This is the ongoing tug of war for school sport that education secretary Michael Gove kicked off in 2010. On one side, the sports lobby is worried about the loss of grassroots Olympic legacy and fears that we are going to produce a nation of inactive children. On the other, government economists talk about financial crises, safeguarding public money and the need to develop a culture where people are less reliant on public services.

Both sides have their complaints. The Government about how during the SSP years, bureaucracies of organisers, planners and managers, took money away from the actual teaching and coaching of PE and sport in schools. Meanwhile, professionals on the ground are wondering who, if not they, will now organise matches and tournaments, arrange visits from external coaches and get children into local sports clubs?

Who will monitor quality, devise programmes to reach disengaged youngsters and stretch the most talented? Who will apply for funding to upgrade facilities? Who will make sure that all children take part, not just those who are already into sport?

The Government's answer to many of these questions has been its School Games – a huge multi-sport event in which, ministers said, children and young people could play proper competitive sport. However, professionals on the ground again are wondering who will get the children to these events, or encourage schools whose headteachers aren't interested in sport to take part?

Lee Holmes, head of PE at Castleford High School in Yorkshire, says that without staff time and funding, PE departments have to put on the extra things that SSPs used to organise in their spare time.

'It's difficult to replace the work that SSPs did with clubs,' he explained. 'The tournaments they organised sparked off a great deal of interest, and without them many children don't get involved.'

One of the biggest worries for schools is the so-called postcode lottery. The fear that without the compulsion of ring-fenced funding attached to national school sports targets, some schools would go their own way. Particularly without the guidance and support that SSPs offered. Dave Crocker, from Brampton Manor School in Essex, asked: 'Should a child's PE and sporting experience be dependent on what an individual PE teacher is interested in or prepared to do, or whether their school is keen on sport?'

The new primary school money is ring-fenced, but there are concerns as to whether primary schools have enough expertise, or the facilities, to make the most of the money. Furthermore, some headteachers will turn to private coaching companies for a quick fix – companies which will run PE lessons for two years, and then disappear when the money runs out.

'If this happens, a school will be back to square one in two years' time,' explained John Steele, chief executive of school sport charity, the Youth Sport Trust. 'We're looking for schools to develop their own capacity to deliver PE and sport.'

Chris Willetts, director of the Tower Hamlets Youth Sport Foundation in east London, believes that primaries will still need help from secondary schools, particularly in the early stages. He explained: 'Some primary schools have had no support for two years, since the SSPs went, and will be starting from scratch, again.'

Mr Willetts, who used to run the local SSP and is still based at Langdon Park School in Tower Hamlets, set up the Foundation after the 2010 funding cuts.

It already provides sports and physical activity specialists for local primary schools, paid for by the schools out of their own budgets, usually through their Pupil Premium fund.

He continued: 'History tells us that you need some sort of infrastructure to make this work. When schools were left to their own devices in the past, it often didn't happen.'

Mr Willetts is also concerned that the new arrangements will cause a divide between primary and secondary schools, with each looking at their own provision and how to pay for it, rather than thinking of designing the best possible physical activity experience.

With no new money coming to secondary schools this September, the Government seems to believe that secondary PE teachers are more than capable of delivering this extra-curricular PE and sport alone.

However, Mr Willetts added: 'Secondary schools need some help too. PE departments won't necessarily have experts in handball, water polo, fencing and sailing – all sports in which Britain won medals at the London Olympics.'

While the Government would point to the Sport England programme to set up community sports clubs and create ties between schools and existing local sports clubs, although Mr Willetts is aware that in some inner city areas it is difficult to find such clubs: 'This is great where there are sports clubs, but in many inner city areas we don't have any.'

In Tower Hamlets, community clubs based in schools but run by external coaches, sourced, paid for and organised by the SSP worked well. After three years, children from one local judo club had even got into the GB squad. 'And these were children who would have never started if left to their own devices.'

And so the tug of war continues. The result: two years of deadlock and a legacy of one of the most successful Olympic Games which is in danger of disappearing. There's a general election due in May 2015. Watch this space for more huffing and puffing.

Crispin Andrews is a freelance writer, former PE Teacher and a sports coach.

16 May 2013

⇨ The above information is reprinted with kind permission from SecEd, part of MA Education Limited. Please visit www.sec-ed.co.uk for further information.

Key facts

⇨ Lesbian and bisexual women are more likely to take part in sport than all women – 44% play sport at least once a week, compared to just over 30%. (page 1)

⇨ Currently 40.9% of men play sport at least once a week, compared to 30.3% of women. (page 3)

⇨ 54.5% of 16- to 25-year-olds (58.0% of 14–25-year-olds) take part in at least one sport session a week, compared to 32.0% of older adults (age 26-plus). (page 3)

⇨ More disabled people are taking part in sport – latest results show 17.8% are playing sport regularly, up from 15.1% in 2005/6. (page 3)

⇨ Around 7.3 million people (16-plus) received sports coaching in 2013/14, while 5.7 million took part in competitive sport. Both activities have declined since 2005/6. (page 3)

⇨ Of the 172 London 2012 medallists who reported back it is estimated that 77% have made at least one school or community appearance. 45% of these London 2012 medallists have already made five or more visits. (page 7)

⇨ Almost 40 million people – more than two thirds of the UK population – viewed the Paralympic Games on TV. (page 12)

⇨ Participation in sport and recreational activity by disabled people increased by 4.2 percentage points in 2012 from 2005/06. (page 13)

⇨ Reports from fans across Europe consistently show that racism exists in football. Italian football tops the league, with 92% of fans saying it exists in Italian football. England is a close second with 91%, with Spanish fans reporting the lowest incidence of racism, with 73% feeling that it exists. (page 15)

⇨ English fans give clubs and players the most credit for combating racism, with 40% feeling that they are doing enough. (page 15)

⇨ 17.1 per cent of LGBT students who participate in team sport are not open to anyone. The main reason for this was that they do not think it is relevant, but 20.5 per cent of those who are not out are worried it might result in verbal or physical abuse on account of homophobia, transphobia or biphobia. (page 16)

⇨ 12.8 per cent of LGBT students do not find facilities, such as showers or changing rooms, inclusive. (page 16)

⇨ Renee Richards played women's tennis in the 1970s and is believed to have been the first transsexual professional athlete. (page 18)

⇨ The most popular sports for women are: 1. Swimming (27.5%); 2. Gym (27.2%); 3. Fitness and Conditioning (14.2%); 4. Athletics (12.1%); and 5. Keepfit Classes (11.1%). (page 21)

⇨ A recent study [about abuse and negative sporting culture], published by researchers from Edinburgh University and the NSPCC, found... reported widespread emotionally harmful treatment (75%) and unacceptable levels of sexual harassment (29%). (page 26)

⇨ [The] launch of the Sideline Bad Behaviour campaign – highlighting the impact of poor behaviour on young players – [found that] 43% have had direct experience of bad behaviour by spectators, 47% said they had witnessed bad behaviour affecting other players [and that] swearing and name calling was the most common form of bad behaviour. (page 28)

⇨ NICE warned that anabolic steroid use is 'relatively widespread' with an estimated 59,000 people aged 16 to 59 using the drug in England and Wales in the last year. (page 30)

⇨ Just in February [2013], Europol identified 380 matches in Europe which were claimed to have been fixed and a further 300 more around the world. Their investigation recognised 425 suspects and 50 people were arrested.

⇨ Out of the 380 suspicious European matches identified in the Europol investigation, more than £8 million was generated in betting profits and more than £2 million was paid in bribes. (page 33)

⇨ BoxeR, a professional gamer, [has accumulated over £320,000 in career prize money]. He has a fan club with 490,000 registered members. A DVD of his winning tactics in 2003 outsold the film *Matrix: Revolutions*. (page 34)

⇨ Thanks to live streaming – allowing fans to watch tournaments over the Internet – eSports has quietly become a multimillion-dollar industry in Europe and the United States, featuring major global events attended by thousands and watched by millions. (page 34)

⇨ Anyone who has suffered concussion should not be left alone for up to 48 hours after their injury. (page 35)

⇨ In 2009/10, more than 90 per cent of pupils had two hours of PE a week and 78 per cent took part in competitive sport. (page 38)

Glossary

Anabolic steroids

'Anabolic steroid' is a blanket term for drugs which mimic the effects of male reproductive hormones, i.e. by boosting muscle growth and protein synthesis. Side effects such as aggression, liver damage and high blood pressure can be very harmful. Some athletes take them illegally in order to improve their performance; people who use these performance-enhancing drugs in excess sometimes don't even view themselves as 'drug addicts', but rather that they are healthy people who are taking pride in their appearance.

Athlete

A highly-trained professional or amateur sportsperson.

Diuretics

A chemical that can be ingested by athletes, increasing the excretion of water from their body during urination. This is done in order to hide banned substances during urine tests, as urine is more diluted. Diuretic use in sporting competitions is illegal.

Doping

The use of performance-enhancing drugs by athletes during sporting competitions. Most of these drugs are illegal and players are required by law to take a drugs test before taking part in competitive events. If it is found that they have taken drugs they will automatically be disqualified from the event, and may also be banned from taking part in any future competitions for a specified period of time.

eSport

Electronic sports (or eSports) refers to competitive gaming events and tournaments (professional gaming). eSports are rapidly gaining popularity and have become a multimillion-dollar industry, featuring major global events attended by thousands and watched by millions. Competitive gaming is claiming a space similar to that of traditional sport and it is a hotly-debated topic as to whether this can be considered a sport or not, and if the players can be called athletes in their own right. This includes video games such as Call of Duty, StarCraft and League of Legends (LoL).

Hooliganism

A popular term in the past for violence at football matches. Match organisers have worked very hard in recent years to combat hooliganism. Police and other security measures are now routinely put in place to control rioting fans, and repeat 'football hooligans' can be banned from travelling abroad to attend games.

Inclusive sport

Sport which is inclusive does not discriminate on the grounds of gender, ethnicity, sexual orientation or disability.

Sport is usually segregated where athletes have a physical difference which makes equal competition difficult – men and women do not generally compete against each other, for example, nor disabled and able-bodied athletes. This is called classification. However, there is no ban on any athlete competing in a separate competition. This is why the term 'sport equity' is sometimes used rather than equality. Athletes should be protected from discrimination and unfair treatment, such as racist and homophobic chanting at football matches.

Match-fixing

Match-fixing is a serious crime and is cheating. This is when someone purposely alters the outcome of a game in exchange for money (a bribe). For example, arranging the use of red and yellow cards or purposely playing poorly in order to throw a game.

Olympic Games

Every four years the Olympic Games are held in a different city around the world. The next summer Olympic Games, which will take place in 2016, are to be held in Rio de Janeiro, Brazil.

Paralympic Games

The Paralympic Games are a series of sporting competitions open to athletes with physical disabilities. They are held immediately following the Olympic Games. Athletes with disabilities including amputations, paralysis and blindness take part in a wide range of competitive sports.

Sideline bad behaviour

When playing sport, children and young people are often subjected to intimidating and abusive behaviour from adults on the side-lines. Nearly half of all young people who experienced or witnessed aggressive behaviour by spectators at sports games said the abuse continued afterwards (for example on the way to the changing rooms or in the car park). This includes experiencing verbal abuse, such as name-calling and swearing, and sometimes even physical abuse, such as being pushed or hit.

Stimulants

A drug which causes a temporary improvement in mental or physical functioning.

Assignments

Brainstorming

⇨ In small groups, discuss what you know about sport in our society. Consider the following points:

- What are all the benefits of participating in sport?

- What are the Olympic and Paralympic games, and why are they important?

- What does the term 'inclusion' mean?

Research

⇨ Investigate match-fixing. Identify some recent high-profile investigations into suspected fixing. What action do you think should be taken against those found guilty of illegally fixing results? Make some notes that detail your findings and discuss with your class.

⇨ Create a questionnaire that will investigate people's experience of racism and violence in sport. Think carefully about the questions you will ask, then distribute the questionnaire and gather your results. Write a short report, analysing your findings, and include some graphs and tables to illustrate your information.

⇨ Do some research to find out about the support available for sportsmen/women who suffer a career-ending injury. Think about psychological/ emotional support as well as physical support and write some notes on your findings.

Design

⇨ Choose a relatively unknown or little-played sport. Create an action plan that will encourage the sport to be more widely played in the UK. Your action plan could include posters, a draft TV ad, etc. Present your action plan to your class.

⇨ Design a poster which highlights why sporting injuries must be taken seriously. Provide some useful information about concussions and how to spot if someone has one.

⇨ Choose one of the articles from this book and create your own illustration that highlights the key themes of the article.

Oral

⇨ Are top athletes born or made? Discuss as a group.

⇨ Stage a debate where one half of the class argues in favour of performance-enhancing drugs and the other argues against them.

⇨ Which public figures do you think embody good sportsmanship? What about bad sportsmanship? Identify the qualities you think a sportsperson should display and discuss with a partner or in small groups.

⇨ Divide your class into two groups: boys and girls. In your groups, discuss why you think there are fewer women than men participating in sport. When both groups have a list of ideas, compare your thoughts and discuss the differences in your opinions.

⇨ Talk to an older family member and ask about their experience of sports or PE at school. How does their experience differ from your own? Make some notes and feedback to your class.

Reading/writing

⇨ Watch *Bend it Like Beckham*. How does this film explore gender stereotypes in sport?

⇨ Choose a film or book that focuses on the life of a well-known sports personality and write a review that analyses the director/author's representation of the main character.

⇨ Read *Hijab and threatens basketball phenom* (pages 24-25). According to the rules of the International Basketball Federation (FIBA), Islamic headscarf, or hijab, is banned in matches. The ban was justified by FIBA as a way to remain religiously neutral. However, very recently Fédération Internationale de Football Association (FIFA) have decided to overturn their ban on headgear. Do some research into the background behind FIFA's decision then write an article or blog post discussing your findings.

⇨ Read *Video games: the sport of the future?* on page 34-36. Write an essay on the rise of eSports and professional gamers. You might want to cover points such as 'can professional gamers be classified as athletes in their own right?' and look into colleges awarding 'athletic scholarships' to gamers.

⇨ Write a letter to your headteacher, explaining why it is important for your school to encourage young people to participate in sports.

⇨ Read *Chapter 3: Issues and controversies*. Choose one of the issues highlighted in this chapter and research it further, then write an article for your school newspaper exploring your findings.

⇨ 'Video games are the sport of the future.' Write an essay either agreeing, or disagreeing, with this statement.

⇨ What would you change about the sports curriculum in your school? Write a proposal that highlights the changes you would make, and explains why.

⇨ Read *Out in Sport* (page 16) and write a summary of the article that could be printed in your school newspaper.

Acknowledgements

The publisher is grateful for permission to reproduce the material in this book. While every care has been taken to trace and acknowledge copyright, the publisher tenders its apology for any accidental infringement or where copyright has proved untraceable. The publisher would be pleased to come to a suitable arrangement in any such case with the rightful owner.

Images

Cover and pages iii, 13, 24 and 27: iStock; page 5 © Gracey; page 6 © Taliesin; page 32 © Jackie Staines.

Illustrations

Don Hatcher: pages 2 & 10. Simon Kneebone: pages 8 & 18. Angelo Madrid: pages 4 & 14.

Additional acknowledgements

Editorial on behalf of Independence Educational Publishers by Cara Acred.

With thanks to the Independence team: Mary Chapman, Sandra Dennis, Christina Hughes, Jackie Staines and Jan Sunderland.

Cara Acred

Cambridge

September 2014